SECRETS TO
MASTERING
THE**WBS**
IN REAL-WORLD PROJECTS
SECOND EDITION

THE MOST PRACTICAL APPROACH TO WORK BREAKDOWN STRUCTURES (WBS)!

LILIANA BUCHTIK, PMP, PMI-RMP

Library of Congress Cataloging-in-Publication Data

Buchtik, Liliana.
  Secrets to mastering the WBS in real-world projects : the most practical approach to work breakdown structures (WBS)! / Liliana Buchtik, PMP, PMI-RMP. -- Second edition.
      pages cm
  Includes bibliographical references.
  ISBN-13: 978-1-62825-033-6 (alk. paper)
  ISBN-10: 1-62825-033-X (alk. paper)
  1. Work breakdown structure. 2. Project management. I. Title.
  HD69.P75B785 2013
  658.4'04--dc23
                              2013037925

ISBN: 978-1-62825-033-6

Published by: Project Management Institute, Inc.
                                14 Campus Boulevard
                                Newtown Square, Pennsylvania 19073-3299 USA
                                Phone: +610-356-4600
                                Fax: +610-356-4647
                                Email: customercare@pmi.org
                                Internet: www.PMI.org

PMI Publications welcomes corrections and comments on its books. Please feel free to send comments on typographical, formatting, or other errors. Simply make a copy of the relevant page of the book, mark the error, and send it to: Book Editor, PMI Publications, 14 Campus Boulevard, Newtown Square, PA 19073-3299 USA.

To inquire about discounts for resale or educational purposes, please contact the PMI Book Service Center.

                      PMI Book Service Center
                      P.O. Box 932683, Atlanta, GA 31193-2683 USA
                      Phone: 1-866-276-4764 (within the U.S. or Canada) or +1-770-280-4129 (globally)
                      Fax: +1-770-280-4113
                      Email: info@bookorders.pmi.org

Dedicated To

First of all, to all my readers who made the First Edition of this book a success:

The project managers looking for better tools, resources, and real-world experiences to make their projects successful and to produce positive business results.

Those who have helped me grow as a person and as a professional in the global project management profession. Those who enriched my understanding and experiences, and learned with me, including my unbelievable coaches and mentors, and my unconditional friends.

My family for their immense love, encouragement, and outstanding support through my biggest challenges and dreams. I owe to you all that I am.

The Second Edition

The First Edition of this book was updated in order to, among other things, align it with PMI's *PMBOK® Guide*—Fifth Edition, to update Chapter 7 to cover the latest versions released in the market related to WBS software, and to add Appendix III with real-world WBS examples.

Acknowledgements

Secrets to Mastering the WBS in Real-World Projects grew out of a series of events that made me realize there was still more to share on this topic. A project like this book is not something I could have achieved alone. This book is the result of a great and talented team of family members, friends, experts, reviewers, editors, designers, companies, and others that collaborated to contribute to it and ultimately, to the global project management profession and community.

I owe special thanks to Dr. Harold Kerzner for reviewing and providing input to my book. Thank you, Federico Loguzzo, for your continued support and overall design guidance. Thank you to the following: Marcelo Torassa, Brandon Conrad, Jim Spiller, Cindy Miller, Osvaldo Ucha, and Laura Toledo for your assistance; my editor, for your fine editing and help; my reviewers for taking the time to read the manuscript and share your thoughts; to my mentors and coaches, and to my publisher, Project Management Institute.

To all of you, my deepest thanks. Without your ideas, time, and contributions this book would not have come to be.

Finally to all my readers, those who made this book a best-seller in the topic, and as a result the need and demand to launch this, Second Edition!

Contents

Figures and Tables

Figures

Tables

Introduction

*I*f you've managed projects, I am sure that you've experienced issues related to the project scope. These include discussions and arguments with the customers about what is and what isn't inside the scope, change requests, and delays, to name a few. It's common to face situations like the one depicted in Figure I.1, where the customer requested a house but expected and wanted a castle; a totally different outcome. It's common to have initial scope definitions that don't match the final project scope. In this example, the customer initially requested a house and the project manager planned for it. The customer was not very clear about the scope at the beginning, nor did the project manager do a good job to understand and properly define the scope. As a result, throughout the project the customer requested more and more things, increasing the scope, timeline, and budget. The castle was delivered with delays, and exceeded the initial budget. Does this sound familiar? How can a project manager plan for a house and deliver a castle? How do you manage scope-related issues? How do you ensure a successful definition of the project scope? What are the tools you should use to help you minimize or avoid situations like this one? — This is what this book is all about. It's about helping you make a difference in your projects and sharing the secrets for you to master the scope management through the use of the work breakdown structure (WBS). You need to carefully plan and manage the scope and its changes to ensure a successful delivery.

Figure I.1 Issues with project scope

In this book, you'll find some of the things that nobody else has written about the WBS. It'll change the way you think about and understand the WBS. The WBS is the cornerstone for successful scope and project management. You can learn to master the WBS and start producing better results in your projects. As you walk through the pages of this book, I'll lead you to discover how you can apply key WBS concepts and techniques to turn your project scope management practices from good to great.

WBS is not yet such a popular term in the project management world like the terms cost, risk, and schedule. In *A Guide to the Project Management Body of Knowledge (PMBOK® Guide)*—Fifth Edition[1] the words risk, cost, and scope are mentioned over 1,000 times, while WBS appears less than 140 times. Perhaps there

---

1   Unless otherwise stated, all material quoted from the *PMBOK® Guide* is referenced to the Fifth Edition (PMI, 2013). The *PMBOK® Guide* is the most globally recognized and ac-cepted project management standard published by Project Management Institute Inc. (PMI).

should be a shift in focus to promote good scope management and effective uses of the WBS to decrease the number of projects that fail or don't meet their goals. In a global research study, PriceWaterhouseCoopers surveyed 200 companies in 30 countries. They found that **scope changes are the second most important and frequent reason for project failure,** as illustrated in **Figure I.2.**

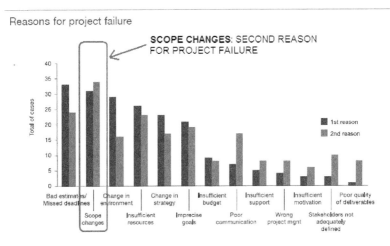

Reasons for project failure

SCOPE CHANGES: SECOND REASON FOR PROJECT FAILURE

Figure I.2 Reasons for project failure[2]

The proof of this statement goes beyond research and statistics. You can search over the Internet and you'll easily find studies[3] that cite several related reasons for project failure including:

- ✻ lack of or poor project planning,
- ✻ changing requirements or specifications, and
- ✻ inadequately trained or inexperienced project managers.

These reasons lead to missed deadlines, exceeded budgets, poor communications, and an inability to meet project requirements, to name a few.

I've used the WBS in real-world projects, as well as proven its benefits to the project, its stakeholders, and to me, the project manager. You can succeed by using this tool, which is simple, but powerful and versatile. I use the WBS in risky and complex projects as well as low-risk and short-term projects. I use it in my country and when I work across continents. I use it with team members who speak my language and

---

2   Evrard, E. and Nieto, A. 2004. *Boosting business performance through program and project management.* Belgium. PriceWaterhouseCoopers. 15.
3   Including the Standish Group, Bull and KPMG Surveys, OASIG Studies and Chaos Reports, and PM Network Magazine articles.

with those project teams that speak different languages. **And the value of a WBS remains the same—it's just an incredible tool that makes a positive impact on your projects when you use it correctly.**

The WBS still doesn't receive the credit it deserves. It's common to find project managers defining a project from a schedule instead of from a well-defined scope and WBS. Some project managers talk about **when** to do something when it's still unclear **what** the project must deliver. You might ask how reliable costs, resources, and time estimates are when the scope is not clear. That would be a valid question.

I presented the *Secrets to Mastering the WBS in Real-World Projects* at an important project management congress where I met Mauricio, who is a project management consultant and certified with the Project Management Professional (PMP)® credential. *"Yours is a very important topic because in this country, we don't know how to use the WBS,"* he said. I smiled. It sounded like a strong comment. I can't say that all the project management professionals in his country don't know how to use the WBS. I know some professionals from that country and other regions of the world who properly use the WBS and obtain positive results in their projects. However, what I believe Mauricio meant to say was that **many, or the majority of the project managers still don't know how to properly apply the WBS in real-world projects**. Some of them still wonder about its benefits. This is one of the reasons why I wrote this book. If you don't use the WBS, this book will help you learn to master it. If you already use the WBS, you'll discover new tips and valuable information and examples to increase your performance and project results.

> This book provides you with **the most practical approach** to using the WBS in real-world projects. By offering you this practical approach, which is different than that of many other texts, I hope to provide you with a unique learning experience.

The most practical approach of this book is evidenced throughout, as it includes more than 200 examples, figures, screenshots, and comparison charts, as well as dozens of real-world stories and lessons learned. You'll see samples of my WBSs and project documents. Most of this book is **written in a simple, questions-and-answers format to keep the discussion at a practical level**. You'll learn the 20 key benefits of properly using the WBS and a proven step-by-step approach to creating valuable WBSs. My intention is for you to easily and quickly understand how to create and use a WBS and to help you drastically enhance your project scope management.

I went on a business trip with work mates from the Project Management Institute (PMI) to attend a conference in Argentina. There, the PMI President and Chief Executive Officer (CEO) at that time, Gregory Balestrero, spoke about project management in the region. Mr. Balestrero is recognized globally as a keynote speaker who addresses many types of professionals from CEOs and government officials to project managers and business people. I liked the speech and told Mr. Balestrero that one of the things I liked about it was that he presented it in a simple way. *"You know, I like to talk* simple *because I want everybody to understand what I say,"* he said. His comment resonated with me. When I decided to write this book, I decided to **keep it simple**, to use simple words and concepts, because my goal is for you to read this book and right after, start mastering the WBS in your projects. I'm convinced that **the WBS is a simple tool.** You just need to know a series of concepts and then put them into practice. However, its simplicity doesn't mean it's trivial. **The WBS is one of the most outstanding project management tools.**

The key differences of this book include:
- its simplicity and new material,
- its how-to and practical approach,
- its alignment with the *PMBOK® Guide*—Fifth Edition,
- its addressing of key current topics like WBS and agile, and global or virtual projects,
- its explanation of the differences between the WBS and the list of activities or schedule,
- its clarification about typical confusions with the WBS,
- the top 20 benefits and a proven step-by-step approach to create a valuable WBS,
- the most comprehensive WBS software tools revision,
- the role of the project management office (PMO) in the WBS,
- first WBS book also available in Spanish,
- its explanation of the different baselines that a project manager must manage, and
- its ability to help you quickly learn what you need to master the WBS, and more.

In addition to learning WBS fundamentals and principles in the first six chapters, in chapter 7 I'll review several WBS software tools and provide a unique comparison chart of these tools as well as a single source where you can examine about thirty more WBS-related software. Chapter 8 tackles the central topic of managing the project scope, scope changes, and scope baseline using the WBS, as well as the role of requirements in scope management. In chapter 9, you'll learn how to manage the schedule and cost baseline, how to integrate the WBS with the schedule and costs, and the benefits of doing that. You'll see in chapter 10 how you can use and maximize the value of the WBS in project communications, risks, human resources, acquisitions, quality, and how the use of colors and images improves communications.

> In my experience, the WBS, more often than not, is the differentiating factor between successful and poor project management. It's a tool for real-world projects, from small to large.

This book is also geared toward global project managers as chapter 11 addresses the WBS and its fit in global, virtual, and multicultural projects.

Chapter 12 presents a rich **discussion about the WBS and scope in agile project management, and the alignment between agile and the PMBOK® Guide.**

Overall, this book will enrich your knowledge and provide you many new and fresh ideas and tips about how to use the WBS in the context of project, program, and portfolio management.

All you need to know and apply to master the WBS is here. **This is the first WBS book aligned with the PMBOK® Guide—Fifth Edition.** It's also aligned with the latest editions of PMI's Practice Standard for Work Breakdown Structures and the Practice Standard for Scheduling, and pulls from other top authors and leaders in the profession. The reason for aligning my book with PMI's global standards is not only because I've proven the value of the application of these standards in my real-world projects, but also because they present generally recognized good practices, concepts, tools, and frameworks that are globally applicable to most projects most of the time. These standards are not created by one organization or agency, or used in one country, or in one or a few industries. They gather universal experience and knowledge from project managers with diverse backgrounds from around the globe. In spite of the said alignment, I don't assume that you are familiar with the *PMBOK® Guide*, so I present the concepts in this book in such a way that **you can understand the WBS even if you are not familiar with the PMBOK® Guide.**

There are several reasons why I wrote this book. Primarily, I wrote it because I felt the need and demand to focus on the practice of using the WBS so that I could share what I've learned with a remarkable practical approach. Secondly, I didn't find in existing literature responses to several questions I had about the WBS and like many other project managers, I didn't have the time to research the answers. So I wrote this book to fill in the gap on how you can quickly apply and put into practice the WBS. Just read the table of contents and you'll see how many questions are presented and you'll easily find the answers in this book.

After one of my presentations about the WBS in a congress, an attendee congratulated me for the way I portrayed WBS topics and examples. She said that my approach filled the gap and clarified confusions about the WBS. This person was the keynote speaker scheduled to close the congress, Janice Thomas, PhD, one of the authors of the widely known book *Researching the Value of Project Management* (PMI, 2008) and program director for the MBA in Project Management of the Athabasca University in Canada. This was more confirmation that I had to write this book and share this information with you. I realized **there is still much confusion about the WBS** and felt compelled to address and it in a clear and simple way.

Finally, I want you to be among that group of project managers who master the WBS and who are able to apply it to be more successful. I hope to convince you how the WBS can help you improve the way you plan and manage your projects. This is **not a theoretical book,** it's written from a project manager, consultant, and trainer to those who somehow practice the profession of project management. **It contains the most current information and practice trends on the WBS**. I'll transmit the things you must know about WBS and you'll know why it's one of my favorite project management tools.

Keep on reading and learn how to use the WBS or improve yourself in its use right away! Don't close this book. It's in your hands to start making a positive impact in your projects right now!

chapter 1

What is the WBS?

We need more than talent to achieve. We need preparation. This applies to everything, from soccer to project management.

reparation comes with learning and then putting what we learned into practice. To master the work breakdown structure (WBS), you need to first learn about it, and then put its concepts into practice in your real-world projects. Otherwise, what you know will remain at a theoretical and unproven level. Before I explain in the next chapter why I believe you should use the WBS and what its benefits are, I'll now define and explain the WBS and its application in programs and portfolios.

WHAT IS THE WBS?

WBS stands for work breakdown structure. The WBS is a structure used to break down or divide the project work, to better manage the project scope, and to define and communicate the scope.

The WBS is not what we have to do (tasks). It's what we have to deliver (deliverables). It's the answer to **what must be delivered** to accomplish the project successfully. It presents the **end vision**, not the means to

accomplish it. It's the answer to **what's inside the project scope**. It gives a full picture of the work to be performed among the stakeholders.

In practical terms, the WBS is what to deliver. It's not the how or when you'll deliver it. **It isn't what to do. It isn't the list of activities** or the schedule that tells you how to execute the work and what tasks you need to deliver the project's end results. It's **a fundamental tool to properly manage the project scope**. It requires you to focus on outcomes, outputs, or, said differently, project deliverables.

These aren't academic or formal definitions. They are the way I define the WBS when I am with my project stakeholders. However, they are supported by global standards as presented below.

According to *The Practice Standard for Work Breakdown Structures,* from PMI, *"the WBS subdivides the project work into smaller, more manageable pieces of work, with each descending level of the WBS representing an increasingly detailed definition of the project work."* [1]

The definition says that the WBS helps you **subdivide the project work into smaller, more manageable pieces**. This means that when you start a project and you are assigned to manage something that is new or complex for you, the WBS helps you understand the work and divide it into smaller pieces that you can manage better. It's the divide-and-conquer approach, which is very good the first time you have to manage a new kind of work.

While I was an information technology (IT) project manager, I remember the first time I was assigned to manage a Web project. I had managed IT projects but not in a Web or Internet platform. When I started defining the project scope, I had many questions about the work. At first, it seemed unmanageable. But using the WBS, I broke down the big picture, the large and complex problem, into pieces of work so I could manage it.

According to the PMBOK® Guide, *"[the WBS is] a **hierarchical decomposition** of the work to be executed by the project team to accomplish the project objectives and create the required deliverables... The WBS organizes and **defines the total scope** of the project"* [2] It also says that the WBS *"is a structured vision of what has to be delivered."*[3]

1   Project Management Institute. 2006. *Practice Standard for Work Breakdown Structures*—Second Edition. Newtown Square, PA: Project Management Institute. 3.
2   Project Management Institute. 2008. *A Guide to the Project Management Body of Knowledge (PMBOK® Guide)*. Newtown Square, PA: Project Management Institute. 126.
3   Project Management Institute. 2008. *A Guide to the Project Management Body of Knowledge (PMBOK® Guide)*. Newtown Square, PA: Project Management Institute. 125.

This means that it is a deliverable-oriented structure.

The definition contains several concepts. First, it states that the WBS is a **deliverable-oriented** structure that defines the project scope. This is a key characteristic of a well-defined WBS as opposed to one that is task or activity oriented. Later, you'll see in Figure 10.1, the differences between tasks and deliverables, but *What is a deliverable?*

A **deliverable** could be a book, a roof in a car construction, a wheel in a bicycle project, a training manual in a training project, a box of printed flyers in a congress project, or a finished wing in an airplane project.

> The WBS is a way to structure different products, results, and/or services that are unique, verifiable, tangible, and measurable. They are called **deliverables.**

Understanding and applying the deliverables concept in the WBS is one of the drivers that will make the difference for your WBSs to create an impact. I'll discuss this more in chapters 5 and 6.

The second formal definition mentions that a WBS is a **hierarchical decomposition** of the project work. Figure 1.1 depicts a basic example of a WBS from a book project with the outcome of a book represented in this hierarchy.

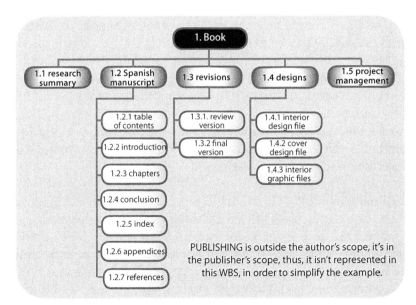

Figure 1.1 Simple WBS example

As you can see, the WBS also provides a way to graphically represent the project scope.

I'll explain this WBS, given this is the first WBS that I present and it could be challenging for you to realize if the components in this WBS depict tasks or deliverables. This is an introductory, simplified WBS. This is the WBS of the author's scope, not the publisher's scope. This doesn't mean that the author of the book will perform all this work alone; it means the author will manage it as this is a self-published book. This WBS example will be used in several sections throughout this book, so let's take a look at its major components before proceeding.

1. Book. This represents the **project's end goal**. This answers the question *what will the project deliver?* The project will deliver a book. The physical book is the outcome. To better manage the book project, the author decomposed (or divided) the book project into its major components, which are: research summary, Spanish manuscript, revisions, designs, and project management.

1.1 Research Summary. This is not the market research related activities. This is a deliverable, a document with an executive summary of the findings and results from the market research done before determining the need and demand for the book. To achieve the market research summary, you'll need to execute tasks. However, while developing a WBS, you don't think what activities or tasks are needed. Instead, you think about the end results that you need to deliver. Once the project scope is defined, you'll start addressing activities for each deliverable.

1.2 Spanish Manuscript. This is the key project deliverable. It's a series of documents with the different components of the book. This manuscript consists of the table of contents, the book introduction, the chapters, the conclusion, the index, the appendices, and the references. Each of the components of the Spanish manuscript is a document that needs to be delivered.

1.3 Revisions. This WBS branch represents the different revisions of the book. It consists of two deliverables. The first deliverable is a manuscript that is ready for input from reviewers. The second deliverable is the manuscript's final version which incorporates feedback from the reviewers and adjustments from the editors. You may wonder why in this WBS, you don't see all the tasks associated with the review and final edition. The answer is that you aren't concerned at this point, during scope definition, about the activities needed to create the book revisions. You just need to be sure to include in the project scope that you'll have a version of the book that's ready for reviewers, and another version, which is the final one, ready to be printed.

1.4 Designs. This component represents the deliverables associated with the designs for the book, meaning the configuration of page size, headings, paper type, the graphic designs that include the figures, images, comparison charts, tables, and diagrams needed for the book. The outcomes of this component will be a series of files created in design software. These files will be inserted into the book manuscript as visual aids. This component doesn't represent the activities that the graphic designer will have to carry out. You just know at this point that the book will have graphic designs in its scope. You also know that as part of the graphic designer's scope, the graphic designer will have to deliver the cover design file (1.4.2 Cover design file), the files for the book interior designs (1.4.1 Interior design files), and the entire book design (1.4.3 Manuscript design file). The manuscript design file is a final deliverable that will be sent to the printing company.

1.5 Project Management. This section represents the work associated with managing the project and will be addressed in chapter 5.

Once you define the scope with a WBS, you can create the project schedule to determine the activities needed to deliver the components defined in the WBS, but the WBS doesn't include tasks. I discuss this in chapter 10.

Let's review a few more things that appeared in the WBS definitions I mentioned earlier.

practical tip

The WBS is to define the project scope and it will be the foundation to define the activities later on in the project schedule.

The first definition mentions that **the WBS has levels and increasing details**. The WBS is broken into different levels and I'll explain that in detail in chapter 5. However, this means that **the WBS allows you to see the work from a very high level (the big picture), down to the lowest level of detail, providing a clear understanding of the scope**.

The definitions also talk about defining the **total project scope**. This indicates that the WBS is not intended to make a nice drawing to capture attention or to show that you use it in your project management practices. The WBS is a tool that ensures you're planning for the total project work—no more, no less.

The WBS needs to include the work related to the interfaces, integrations, or dependencies between projects.

> The WBS must not include anything that isn't part of the project scope.

An example of interfaces and integrations is two different software projects that exchange information. Project A will create a corporate website. Project B will create a website to track customer orders. Project A will integrate with project B by providing a link in the corporate website so customers can track their orders. There has to be a coordination and integration between the corporate website and the system to track orders.

An example of dependencies is, project A will need a deliverable from project B. Project A's WBS needs to define the work to coordinate and integrate with the deliverables that will receive from project B. Project A is an educational project where new techniques will be taught through the use of computers especially designed for children with disabilities. Project B is responsible to design, build, and deliver the special computers. Project A will integrate with project B and project B will provide the computers as inputs to project A.

The WBS significantly increases the chances of success, good planning, and execution if early in the project you have a WBS with a good definition of the total scope. As the definition says, the WBS helps to accomplish the objectives of the project.

There's a popular saying among project managers. *"What isn't in the WBS, is outside of scope."* I use this phrase often. Keep this phrase in mind and use it! It'll remind both your stakeholders and you how important the WBS is. Chapters 3 and 5 will continue to define and explain the WBS.

See **Appendix III** for four WBS of real-world projects. Those include electrical and architecture/construction projects.

WHAT ARE THE PROGRAM WBS AND PORTFOLIO WBS?

Since I've defined the WBS for projects, you may wonder what the WBS for a program or portfolio is like. The same concepts, tools, techniques, and examples apply to a project WBS, program WBS, and portfolio WBS.

The difference between a project WBS and a program or portfolio WBS is in the content. For example, a project WBS will have the work and deliverables for a project, while a program WBS will present the work of the program as a whole, like a set of projects.

Another difference is who the responsible is for the WBS. In a project, the project manager is responsible for the project WBS. In a program, the program manager is responsible for the program WBS. The same applies to portfolio management. With these minor differences noted, I'll talk about the WBS of a project throughout this book. However, all the concepts presented are also applicable to WBSs for programs and portfolios.

Now that you learned what a WBS is and that you are familiar with a simple WBS example, in the next chapter I'll share why you should use the WBS and what its top 20 benefits are.

chapter 2

Why Should You Use the WBS? Top 20 Benefits

"Practice isn't the thing you do once you're good. It's the thing you do that makes you good." - Malcolm Gladwell

You often hear about how projects fail or don't meet their objectives. As shown in the Introduction, one of the reasons for this is because **many times, there isn't a clear understanding of the project scope and what has to be managed.** As a result, the project faces too many scope changes. In other words, many project managers don't use the WBS or don't use it correctly. The WBS is known in theory but not practiced too widely. As Malcolm Gladwell said, *"Practice isn't the thing you do once you're good. It's the thing you do that makes you good."*[1] For you to see positive or improved results in your projects, you need to start using the WBS. You need to practice with it until you master it and you are able to observe its positive results. I'll discuss the top 20 benefits of using the WBS and show you how the WBS can improve your project results.

1 Gladwell, M. 2008. *Outliers*. New York: Little Brown. 42.

WHAT ARE THE TOP 20 BENEFITS OF USING THE WBS?

 1 – UNDERSTAND WORK AT EARLY STAGES

Oftentimes, at the project initiation, the project team doesn't have a good understanding of the project scope—products, services, and results. Generally speaking, when you begin a project, for different reasons there could be a high level of uncertainty added to the pressure placed on the project manager to show a plan as soon as the project is initiated. I've seen project managers assigned to a project on Monday, and on Wednesday, their superiors ask for the project schedules and the plan! There is so much anxiety to see schedules and plans at the project initiation stage when planning has not even begun. As a result, teams run into the project execution without having spent the necessary time understanding the work needed to implement the project successfully. Oftentimes, the executives don't understand that to create a useful schedule, you need first to understand the project scope. Thus, during execution, you realize that you haven't identified, budgeted, and scheduled some of the tasks. What is the consequence? You need to start negotiating to decrease the scope or quality, to increase the budget, or any number of unexpected and unplanned things.

One of the most important benefits of a well-defined WBS is that **it helps you to really understand all the project work in the early stages of the project**. It helps in discussions with stakeholders to determine the work that is required and ensures that you aren't forgetting or missing anything.

 2 – AVOID UNCONTROLLED CHANGES

A good WBS helps you avoid uncontrolled changes, which are known as **scope-creep**. The clearer you define the scope before project execution, the higher the chances are for you to succeed as there will be less need for change requests. Sometimes a project starts to deviate from its scope very slowly. Without realizing it, at some point, you can't control the scope changes any more. With a well-defined WBS, a WBS that is created among experts, the project team, and stakeholders, you have more chances to capture all the work needed, thus reducing the number of scope change requests.

3 – DELIVER WHAT IS EXPECTED

The *Practice Standard for WBS* stresses that *"the WBS also establishes the framework for managing the work to its completion."*[2] The WBS helps you deliver what the project was created for, the outcomes and deliverables described in the scope statement. When you define the scope in the WBS, the team is able to work until all the deliverables are successfully completed, and only the approved deliverables are completed. It helps to ensure that the team is headed in the right direction, and only focused on what is needed.

 ## 4 – UNDERSTAND AREAS WITH LIMITED UNDERSTANDING

In one of the projects I managed, one important piece of work had to do with a procurement process to purchase a Web conferencing system. This is a system to work and interact virtually with other individuals by using tools such as presentations, whiteboards, surveys, notes, webcams, etc. I had never purchased such a system before. As a result, I created a first draft of the scope of work and WBS for that piece, and then looked for advice from other people both internal and external to the organization that had experience with Web conferencing solutions. That was one of the most successful procurement processes I ever conducted. The WBS helped us to understand the areas of work where we initially lacked understanding, where we needed to learn more, research more, or get an expert. It also helped to clarify the relationship among the different components or deliverables. It can help you do the same.

 ## 5 – VISUALIZE INTERNAL AND EXTERNAL WORK

The WBS helps to identify what is the scope that will be made in-house and what work will be acquired externally. What will be performed by your team, and what the providers will be responsible for. I further discuss this in chapter 10.

---

2   *Practice Standard for WBS*—Second Edition. 1.

6 – VISUALIZE PROJECT BOUNDARIES AND MANAGE COMPLEXITIES

The WBS helps the stakeholders understand and visualize in a clear and easy way, what is inside of scope and what is not. It provides a clear vision of the project outcomes and helps understand all of the project work, and only the work needed. When stakeholders have questions regarding what is in scope or not, they can refer to the WBS. A stakeholder once contacted me requesting my team to publish an advertisement in a magazine for a promotion that he understood was in scope. After we reviewed the WBS together, we realized that the request was not in the approved scope.

The WBS is also *"…one of the primary methods for managing complex projects"[3]* because you can decompose the project scope into simpler components. This is a key benefit. I'll fully discuss this aspect throughout this book and especially in chapter 5.

7 – PROVIDE A BASELINE FOR SCOPE CHANGE CONTROL

The WBS is the baseline for scope change control as I'll discuss in chapter 9. What does this mean? It means that the WBS guides you through the process of reviewing and approving, or rejecting requests to change the project scope. The WBS is a guide to determine how to react or face the requests for scope changes. Figure 1.1 represented a WBS with the Spanish version of a book inside of scope. However, there wasn't indication of deliverables to publishing the book in Chinese or Portuguese. There wasn't indication of translation deliverables, so translations in other languages outside Spanish are not within scope. You can rely on the WBS to prove deliverables that are not listed there. If the customer wants to add translations to the project, you'll need to go through the scope change control process.

8 – ASSIGN AND EXPLAIN THE WORK

The WBS helps to assign the work. It helps the project manager or leader to explain what the work is for each WBS component. Each

---

3   *Practice Standard for WBS*—Second Edition. 7.

component within the WBS has a person assigned to it. That person is responsible to ensure that the pieces of work will be achieved. This is illustrated in Figure 2.1 where Martin is responsible for all the deliverables regarding interior designs. If you have any questions about those deliverables, you can talk with Martin. It doesn't matter if Martin will work alone on that or if he will have a team working with him. He is the ultimate responsible for that work. The same way, Federico will deliver the file with the cover design and Mark and Tina are responsible for the work associated with the promotional items.

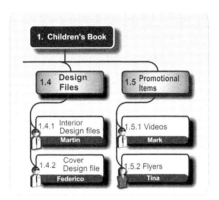

Figure 2.1 WBS element responsible

In this example, the project manager uses the WBS to discuss with the graphic designers what's inside the project scope regarding the cover and interior design files. This will also allow the stakeholders to understand what the outcomes are that Martin and Federico are responsible for—the definition of their scope.

 ## 9 – ENHANCE PROJECT PLANNING

A well-defined WBS has a great impact in the project planning. Why? Because once you have a good WBS, it's easier to identify and define the project activities. It's easier to identify the budget needed as you can easily estimate the cost of the WBS components. It also helps to estimate the duration of each component and the resources needed to implement them. The WBS **helps you plan better and faster**.

In chapter 9 there is a comprehensive discussion about the WBS as an input to project plans and how it positively influences the project planning.

10 – AVOID REPLANNING AND DETECT EARLY WARNINGS

Related to the second benefit discussed, the WBS assists in minimizing the need to replan the project. It helps you avoid missing deadlines and exceeding the approved budgets. It's useful in identifying early warnings in the project when it's less costly to take preventive actions or implement corrective actions. The WBS is a key input to many project management processes as defined in the *PMBOK® Guide*. I discuss this in greater detail from chapters 9 to 11.

11 – BUILD STRONG FOUNDATIONS FOR ACQUISITIONS

The WBS is a good foundation for successful statements of work, contracts, and acquisitions. When you have a good understanding of the products, services, or results that you need to acquire, you are in a better position to explain that in a request for proposal. This benefit and how the WBS relates to acquisitions is discussed in chapter 10.

12 – IMPROVE COMMUNICATIONS

The WBS is very useful to communicate project information to stakeholders, especially information related to project scope. You can also communicate other aspects of the project beyond scope as I'll discuss in chapter 10. In chapter 10 I'll also introduce tips regarding the use of colors and techniques to enhance the presentation of the WBS to highlight different aspects of the project. Through the WBS, the stakeholders gain visibility into a textual, tabular, or graphical representation (tree structure) of the work, deliverables, and products involved in the project scope.

In more complex projects, the WBS is good to communicate the project complexity. I've managed projects whose complexity or dimension was initially underestimated, and representing all the scope in the WBS has helped my team to communicate the complexity involved as well as the project dimension.

13 – ACHIEVE A COMMON UNDERSTANDING OF THE WORK

The stakeholders can provide feedback about the scope and WBS and you can all clarify everyone's understanding about the work, reaching a common expectation of the project's outcomes. This avoids what Figure 2.2 represents—having a customer expect one outcome, and having all the different stakeholders think something different.

The scope as described by the sponsor

The scope as understood by the project manager

The scope recommended by consultants

The scope as expected by the customer

The scope as documented by the analyst

The scope needed for the project

Figure 2.2 Different interpretations of the project scope[4]

14 – IMPROVE PROJECT REPORTING

You can extend the value of the WBS and apply it beyond its typical uses. For example, you can use the WBS for project reporting. You can report progress against the WBS by showing which deliverables are complete, which ones are in progress, which ones have not yet

4   Tractor image from http://www.igortractors.com.uy (accessed June 2009). Copyright of Igor Tractors.

started, as well as other information. The WBS is used to *"provide the project management team with a framework on which to base project status and progress reports."*[5] Chapter 10 expands on this benefit. The WBS is not only useful during the project initiation and planning; it's also useful throughout the project life cycle.

15 – GAIN STAKEHOLDERS' BUY-IN

Like anyone else, project teams and stakeholders like to be involved in key decisions that affect them. This means that they need to be involved in the scope definition, and you need their buy-in. Generally, the WBS is completed through the joint efforts of the project manager, project team, and key stakeholders. As a result, you get the stakeholders' buy-in for the work definition. The WBS becomes a representation of their input. In my projects, for example, as the project manager, I create the first draft of a proposed WBS. I complete the WBS as much as I can and then I start reviewing it with the project team. When needed, I also incorporate input and advice from experts. When I have a business analyst on my team, I work with the business analyst on the WBS from the very beginning. I often work on the WBS with my program manager or the manager of the Program Manager Office (PMO) as they provide valuable expertise. After those revisions with the team and/or experts, you go through different versions of the WBS with the stakeholders until you achieve a final version that is understood by everybody. After that, the WBS is approved and becomes the scope baseline for the project.

16 – MONITOR, MEASURE AND CONTROL WORK BETTER

The WBS serves as a tool to monitor, measure, and control the project. The WBS is a valuable communications tool and by reporting and communicating key information it's also serving as a tool to monitor the project. In chapter 10 I'll present examples of ways in which the WBS helps to monitor the project as well as discuss its relationship to other project management areas like risks and procurement. The WBS also assists in measuring and controlling the project. For example, the WBS helps you to evaluate the defined work against the accomplished work.

---

5   *Practice Standard for WBS*—Second Edition. 1.

17 – INSPIRE CONFIDENCE AND GAIN CREDIBILITY

I've discovered that a well-written WBS presented to the stakeholders at the beginning of the project gives them the confidence that the project team has gone through a thorough understanding of the work involved, thus increasing the chances of success. It's especially good for the project sponsors to see the WBS to gain a good understanding of the scope and deliverables. Seeing a good definition of the scope **allows the sponsors and customer to feel that the project is in good hands** and this builds the project team's credibility.

18 – IMPROVE FUTURE PROJECTS

A good WBS also can be used as a template for future similar projects and as a checklist of work needed. You can use the WBS to gather lessons learned, including what the team has learned about the work that was defined and executed, what went well, and what can be improved in the future. I once managed a project where six months before the project's end date, we had already scheduled a meeting with the stakeholders to conduct a post-project review to have a lessons-learned discussion. This is always a great practice. The WBS is one of the key inputs for those kinds of meetings. I'll discuss about the use of templates with the WBS in chapter 6.

19 – COMPARE SCOPE AMONG PROJECTS

Another benefit of the WBS is to compare the scope of work between two or more projects in a program. In companies where dozens or hundreds of projects are being executed with many different departments and stakeholders, you run the risk of potentially overlapping or having redundancy of scope among projects. Thus, for a program manager, it's important to make sure that there aren't two projects defining and executing the same work. One way to identify redundancy is to compare the WBS of two projects. In two related projects I had in the past, we realized there was a miscommunication about some documentation work that was planned to be executed in two projects. By identifying the duplicated work in each WBS, it was clarified which of those projects was going to execute that deliverable and it was removed from the other project's WBS.

 ## 20 – INTEGRATE SCOPE WITH TIME AND COST

This is **the KEY benefit**—having the possibility to link the WBS with the schedule and costs. This allows you to determine if all the defined and approved scope has an associated plan and if you haven't planned anything that you shouldn't (as it's not inside of the approved scope). Also, the WBS *"provides the basis for integrating and assessing schedule and cost performance."*[6] In chapter 9, I present a comprehensive discussion of this benefit.

Figure 2.3 shows an image with a summary of the key twenty benefits presented about the WBS. This doesn't mean that these are the only benefits. There are many more benefits in addition to the twenty that I presented; however, as a starting point, I provided them. You'll find more benefits throughout this book.

> **practical tip**
>
> *Consider working on the WBS and the project charter simultaneously so you get an early and accurate representation of the capacity of the project.*

Even though the project charter is an input to the WBS, I've worked on the project charter and WBS almost in parallel. It has proven to be a successful practice to work on the WBS at the very start of the project and to include at least a high-level representation of the WBS as an appendix to the project charter, even though it's not technically part of a charter. However, the project charter requires a summary budget, a summary milestone schedule, and other requirements. **Including the WBS in the charter increases the accuracy of the capacity of the project.**

---

6   *Practice Standard for WBS*—Second Edition. 7.

TOP 20 BENEFITS

1. understand work at early stages

2. avoid uncontrolled changes

3. deliver what is expected

4. understand areas with limited understanding

5. visualize internal and external work

6. visualize project boundaries and manage complexities

7. provides a baseline for sope change control

8. assign and explain work better

9. enhance project planning

10. avoid re-planning and detect early warnings

11. build strong foundations for acquisitions

12. improve communications

13. achieve a common understanding of project work

14. improve project reporting

15. gain stakeholder's buy-in

16. monitor, measure and control work better

17. inspire confidence and gain credibility

18. improve future projects (templates, documentation)

19. compare scope among projects

20. integrate scope with time and cost

Figure 2.3 Summary of Bg® WBS Top 20 Benefits

chapter 3

What Are the 4 Typical Confusions about the WBS?

"The beginning of knowledge is the discovery of something we do not understand." - Frank Herbert[1]

*T*here's a list of real stories I could share with you about moments when I talked with different professionals about the WBS and realized they were very confused about the true concept and value of it. Now that I've summarized some of the benefits of the WBS, I'll present the four most common misconceptions about the WBS that I've observed among project managers and stakeholders. I'll share these misconceptions by recounting real-life stories.

---

1   The Quotations Page. www.quotationspage.com/quote/26173.html (accessed August 2009)

STORY 1: CONFUSING THE WBS WITH WORK SEQUENCING

I once visited the exhibitor's area of an important project management event and found a local software company selling project management software that I wasn't familiar with. I asked the person in the booth about the software. *"Does your software implement the WBS?" "Sure,"* the exhibitor answered. When I asked to see it, the exhibitor started to show me the graphical structure representation of the WBS, which looked nice, and she started to talk about how they implement the concepts. Up to that point, everything was perfect. Then, she said, *"…in the WBS you can see the dependencies, the tasks and their relationships. You can see everything in the WBS!"* When I heard this, I thought, *"Oh no! Here it comes again! This person is confused about what a WBS is!"* She didn't understand the difference between the WBS and the schedule. The exhibitor was talking about tasks, dependencies, and task relationships in a WBS but **a WBS is NOT a way to show or represent tasks or dependencies.** In chapter 9 I'll clarify the difference between a WBS and a list of activities or schedule.

STORY 2: BEING TRAINED WITH OLD WBS CONCEPTS

While I was writing this book, a known North American university was offering a video about the WBS. I wanted to watch it, given that university has a master's degree program in project management and I was interested to know about their WBS training. To my disappointment, when they presented the definitions and concepts about the WBS, they were based on concepts from almost 30 years ago—concepts defined since the early 1960s and included in the *PMBOK®* in 1987 when the WBS knowledge was not as rich as what is available today.

At that time, **almost 30 years ago, the WBS was defined with a task-oriented approach** rather than a deliverable-oriented approach. What do I mean by that? In 1987 the *PMBOK®* defined the WBS as *"a task-oriented family tree of activities."* However, in 1996, the definition changed. In 1996, the *PMBOK® Guide* defined the WBS as *"a deliverable-oriented grouping of project elements which organizes and defines the total project scope."*

Can you see the difference? In 1987 and before then, the project management community was talking about **task orientation** and activities, but in 1996 it started to talk about **deliverable orientation**!

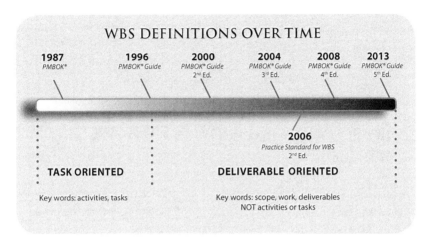

Figure 3.1 WBS definitions over time

Since then, the *PMBOK® Guide* editions published in 1996, 2000, 2004, 2008, and 2013, have consistently defined the WBS as a deliverable-oriented structure, not as a task-oriented structure—as shown in Figure 3.1.

However, I still find training programs and trainers teaching the WBS as a task-oriented structure or as a structure to define processes. They're training concepts from over 25 years ago, and haven't updated their materials to the new approaches that have been validated and more globally accepted for almost 20 years. They still present the WBS as a way to represent tasks, and this is confusing. The WBS is NOT a way to represent tasks.

The above mentioned video defined the WBS as *"a method for identifying and organizing **all the tasks** needed to achieve the project's requirements."* This is a good definition for 1987 or before then, but **nowadays, the globally accepted definition is different.**

The *PMBOK® Guide* and the *Practice Standard for WBS* don't mention the tasks in their WBS definitions any-more. In 1987, the words "activity" and "task-oriented" were removed from the WBS definition.

The last time when the *PMBOK® Guide* used the word "task" in the WBS definition was in 1987. Later editions talk about "work" or "scope," and the whole approach is oriented to that now. But WBSs still exist with labels like "acquire materials," which aren't to describe deliverables but tasks. Such descriptions shouldn't be included in the WBS. This is confusing for project managers. Even today, many receive training that is outdated and not very valuable for creating a WBS that can make a positive impact in our work.

STORY 3: CONFUSING THE WBS WITH THE SCHEDULE

I received an e-mail from a project manager who sent me a Gantt chart and the e-mail's subject read: *"Feedback required to the WBS."* I opened the e-mail. It had a Gantt chart, not a WBS. How could I have provided input to the WBS if what I received wasn't a WBS? Instead, it was a list of activities from a file in a scheduling software. This is another example that not every project manager understands what a WBS is. However, some of them use the term, thinking they know what it means. This is why, in this book, I specifically address this confusion, to clarify the difference between a list of activities and a WBS. Figure 9.1 and Table 9.1 in chapter 9 will depict those key differences.

The WBS doesn't represent tasks; it focuses on deliverables and outcomes. **Listing the tasks is something related to project time management, not related to project scope management**. The *PMBOK® Guide* talks about how to manage project time and presents various processes related to the project schedule, which are different from the processes related to managing the scope.

STORY 4: CONFUSING THE WBS WITH AN ORGANIZATIONAL BREAKDOWN STRUCTURE

This final real story addresses the confusion that some project managers have by thinking that any kind of graphical structure, representation, or breakdown, is a WBS. For example, a project manager sent the stakeholders the graphic in Figure 3.2 labeling the communication as *"WBS and reporting structure."*

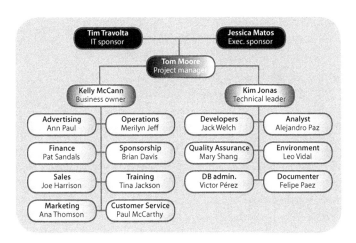

Figure 3.2 Example of what is NOT a WBS

When I opened the file, I realized that it wasn't a WBS. The project manager was confused. Why wasn't it a WBS? Basically it didn't fit the WBS definition. You can check in chapter 6 on the steps to create a valuable WBS and you'll quickly realize that this wasn't a WBS. In the next section you'll learn that this is an Organizational Breakdown Structure (OBS) for the project. You could use this as a reporting structure, but you can't call it a WBS.

Based on this final story, I'll now present some graphical structures that could lead to confusion. I'll clarify what each of them is so you can see how they differ from a WBS.

> Remember that not every graphical structure, representation, or breakdown, is a WBS.

AVOID CONFUSION WITH THE RBS, OBS, CBS, AND BOM

There are different diagrams that due to their appearance could lead you to think that they are a WBS. The most widely known and used are briefly presented below so you can learn what they are to avoid confusing them with a WBS.

- Risk Breakdown Structure (RBS)
- Resource Breakdown Structure (RBS)
- Organizational Breakdown Structure (OBS)
- Contract Breakdown Structure (CBS)
- Cost Breakdown Structure (CBS)
- Bill of Materials (BOM)

After presenting each of them, you'll note that these structures are NOT WBSs, as they don't define the project scope or its work. They are all very useful and you should considering using them, however, you shouldn't use them as a WBS. I'll explain each of these structures.

The **Risk Breakdown Structure (RBS)**[1] is used to show the different areas or **risk categories** that the project may have. It helps to identify risks per category, for example, political risks, environmental risks, economic risks, technology risks, stakeholder's risks, or contractual risks. It's used as a checklist to help identify potential risks within a project.

Figure 3.3 depicts examples of risks per each category for the Bg New Website Project, for example, project management risks, technical risks, training risks, and internal and external risks. It shows a category for unforeseeable risks which are those you can't foresee at this point. The three major areas of risks—very tight deadlines, politics, and technical resources shortage—are highlighted because they are of higher concern for the project manager in this project.

---

1   Note: the abbreviation RBS is used for both the Risk Breakdown Structure and the Resource Breakdown Structure. However, these structures are not the same concept. This comment also applies to the abbreviation CBS, used here for Contract Breakdown Structure or Cost Breakdown Structure

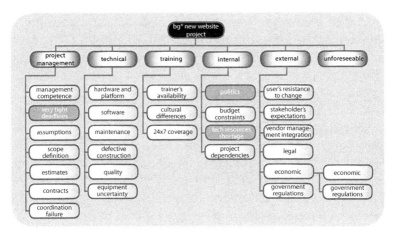

Figure 3.3 Risk Breakdown Structure (RBS)

As you can see, this is NOT a WBS, work decomposition, or definition of project scope. This is a way to structure different categories or risks. It's a great tool to help in identifying and managing risks.

The **Resource Breakdown Structure (RBS)** is a hierarchical classification of the **resources** that you need to accomplish the project. Figure 3.4 represents such a structure and describes how the project resources are organized.

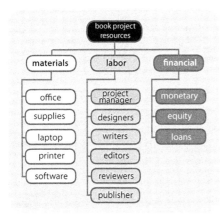

Figure 3.4 Resource Breakdown Structure

Figure 3.4 presents the human and material resources that you have, or that you need to obtain, for the project. It helps to assign resources to work packages by using it in conjunction with the WBS.

For example, you could ask: *"What resources do you need to achieve the Spanish Manuscript deliverable illustrated in the WBS shown in Figure 1.1?"* The project may need at least one writer from the labor resources and one laptop, one printer, and an office from the materials resources. There are different ways to group or categorize the resources depending on the project.

The **Organizational Breakdown Structure (OBS)** is an organizational chart that shows the hierarchical structure of the project's organization. It represents the departments and functions involved, the lines of report and the chain of command . While the WBS shows the hierarchy among deliverables, the OBS shows the **hierarchy of people and groups** and the units responsible for the WBS components. Figure 3.5 presents an OBS.

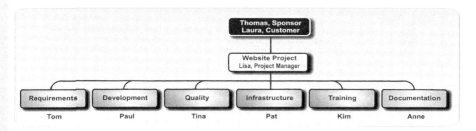

Figure 3.5 Organizational Breakdown Structure (OBS)

This OBS represents that Lisa is the project manager for the website project, and she reports to Thomas—the project sponsor—and to Laura—the customer. The project is organized with six teams whose functions and leaders are shown. For example, Tom is responsible for the requirements, Paul is responsible for the software development team, Tina is the quality assurance leader, and Pat is responsible for the project infrastructure.

There's some, but not much of a relationship between the WBS and the OBS, other than relating the work packages[2] to the project's organization. The OBS is good to show the project teams and organization but it does NOT represent the project scope of work.

The **Contract Breakdown Structure (CBS)** shows a breakdown of project's **contracts and subcontracts**. Figure 3.6 shows the con-

2   Work packages are the lowest-level WBS components, where the work is planned. They will be discussed further in chapter 5.

tracts needed in a website project. For each of those contracts, the provider responsible for them is identified. Some responsibilities could be determined at a later stage of the project. You can present the Contract Breakdown Structure at a more detailed level to be more accurate with the scope of work. However, for our purposes, the example should suffice. For further details, see "How Do You Use the WBS in Acquisitions" in chapter 10.

1. Website project - CONTRACTS
    1.1. Website design files
        1.1.1. Home page files - *Inventive, Inc.*
        1.1.2. Other pages files - *Inventive, Inc.*
    1.2. Website modules - *Developing, Inc.*
    1.3. Videos - *ABC Productions, Inc.*
    1.4. Newsletters - *MarkMail, Ltd.*
    1.5. Hosting - *TelecSouth, Inc.*

Figure 3.6 Contract Breakdown Structure (CBS)

The **Cost Breakdown Structure (CBS)** represents the breakdown of the project **costs** as shown in Figure 3.7. You can use it in conjunction with the WBS to map the estimated costs. Work can be grouped by cost center using this structure.

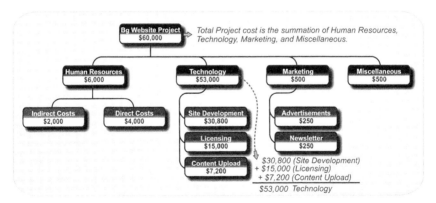

Figure 3.7 Cost Breakdown Structure (CBS)

This figure portrays the cost breakdown for the bg® Website Project whose total cost is $60,000. It shows the composition of the $60,000 and what the corresponding amount is for human resources, technology, marketing, and miscellaneous. The CBS will be at a high level, or will have initial costs at the beginning of the project, during Initiation and early Planning. Those costs will be refined as more information becomes available and as you obtain more accurate costs. This is NOT a WBS. It's a breakdown of project costs. In chapter 9, I'll discuss "How You Can Link the WBS with Costs".

Bill of Materials (BOM) *"is a list of the raw materials, sub-assemblies, intermediate assemblies, sub-components, components, parts and the quantities of each needed to manufacture an end item (final product)."*[3] An example is shown in Figure 3.8.

BILL OF MATERIALS (BOM)				
Item	Component	Material	Impact	Unit
Building - Structural concrete	Beam	Cement	0.34	Ton
		Coarse aggregate	1.25	Ton
		Sand	0.7	Ton
		Steel reinforcement	0.12	Ton
	Column	Cement	0.34	Ton
		Coarse aggregate	1.25	Ton
		Sand	0.7	Ton
		Steel reinforcement	0.1	Ton
	Foundation	Cement	0.34	Ton
		Coarse aggregate	1.25	Ton
		Sand	0.7	Ton
		Steel reinforcement	0.9	Ton

Figure 3.8 Bill of Materials (BOM)

The BOM is a hierarchical structure with the top level representing the finished product. Some of the fields or information often found in a BOM is the item number, description, and quantity. There are also other fields like price, material, and source that can be used. You can link the BOM with the WBS by adding a WBS ID column to the BOM. The WBS ID column will indicate which is the WBS component associated to each item in the BOM. The WBS ID will be discussed in chapter 5.

---

3   Reid, R. Dan and Sanders, Nada R. 2002. *Operations Management*. John Wiley & Sons. 457–458. Monk, Ellen and Wagner, Bret. 2009. *Concepts in Enterprise Resource Planning*. Course Technology Cengage Learning. 97-98. Quoted online at www.wikipedia.org. Author bolded certain words in original quote for the purpose of this book.

It's not the purpose of this book to discuss other structures, just to present a high-level explanation of the most common ones that could lead to confusion with the WBS.

STRUCTURE TYPES COMPARISON CHART

This is a comparison chart of the different types of graphical structures discussed. It is useful to have a quick picture of the common structures together in order to identify their main differences.

bg® STRUCTURE TYPES COMPARISON CHART		
Structure Acronym	Structure Name	Representation of
WBS	Work Breakdown Structure	**Work**, scope, deliverables
RBS	Risk Breakdown Structure	**Risk** categories
RBS	Resource Breakdown Structure	**Resources** (human and materials) needed and its organization
OBS	Organizational Breakdown Structure	Project's **organization**: people, groups, departments and functions involved, as well as reporting relationships
CBS	Contract Breakdown Structure	**Contracts** and subcontracts
CBS	Cost Breakdown Structure	Project **costs**
BOM	Bill of Materials	Item **materials**, assemblies, components, and/or parts.

Table 3.1 bg® Structure Types Comparison Chart

Remember, not all structures or graphical representations are a WBS. The WBS isn't a drawing tool to sell a project or proposal. It's a valuable tool primarily to define and communicate the project work.

Concluding this chapter, I remind you of the four stories I shared that illustrate the most common pitfalls and misunderstandings about the WBS. The WBS is not a structure to show how the work is sequenced, and it isn't supposed to be used to represent tasks. The WBS presents project deliverables, outcomes, and results. Further it isn't the project schedule, although it can be integrated and linked with the schedule, as I'll discuss in later chapters. Finally, not every graphical structure or representation is a WBS. Structures like the RBS, OBS, CBS, and BOM are all valid structures and concepts to help you better manage your projects; however, they don't represent the project scope of work. All or most of these structures can be used in combination with the WBS.

In the next chapter I'll respond to some important questions to begin setting the stage and understanding of the WBS and its applicability.

chapter 4

What Are the Key Questions to Understanding the WBS?

One of the characteristics of smart people and innate learners is that they are not afraid of asking questions, and they listen carefully to the answers.

*I*f you've considered using the WBS, or if you're being introduced to it with this book, I'm sure you've asked yourself several questions— simple but important questions. It was probably difficult to find a direct and short answer to each of them. You may have wondered what if you don't use the WBS. After all, if not everybody uses it, why should you use it? You also may have asked how applicable the WBS is? Can you use it in any industry, or in any kind of projects despite its size, complexity, and other factors? After thinking about all these question, you decided to start using the WBS to prove to yourself if it's really valuable. But then more questions arise. How should you start? Who should create it?

re's a natural list of questions that surface as you start thinking
ut how to better manage the scope of your project and how to
properly use the WBS. This chapter will answer a first set of questions
aimed to help you understand the WBS. Chapter 5 will continue this
discussion and answer questions that go beyond those, that will
begin to help you master it. After reading this chapter, I hope you
convince yourself to give the WBS a try. This chapter will address the
following questions:

-
- What if you don't use the WBS?
- Can you apply the WBS to any project?
- When do you create and use the WBS?
- Who should create the WBS?
- How do you create the WBS?
- How should you update the WBS?
  What is the PMO's role in the WBS?

WHAT IF YOU DON'T USE THE WBS?

If you don't use the WBS, you may lose the opportunity to improve
the way you manage not only the project scope but also other areas
of your projects. Managing a project without a WBS is like going on
a trip to an unknown place without an idea of what will be found at
the destination.

These are some of the things that are likely to happen if you don't
use a valuable WBS:

-
  The time you spend planning your project will be longer
  because you'll start discovering pieces of work that you
- missed as the project progresses. This is so typical!
  The quality of your project plan will be poor or not as
- good as it could be if you had used a valuable WBS.
  The estimating process (cost, durations, and resources)
  will be more difficult, as the WBS won't be there to
  provide the valuable input that it was created to provide.

* Your stakeholders' expectations will be harder to manage because they won't have a good understanding of the project work. This will be even more serious for larger, global, or multicultural projects where different languages could add communication challenges.

* You run the risk of needing to alter your project baseline several times, reviewing, evaluating, and approving or rejecting scope change requests. It'll be more difficult to control scope changes.

* You could run into budget overruns as you miss work that you didn't budget. You'll need to request additional funds. This also takes time, and what if there are no more funds available?

* It'll be harder for you to realize whether not all the approved project scope was planned, and if you've planned work outside of the approved scope. This is explained in chapter 9.

* It may not be clear who's accountable for the different pieces of work, and as a result, the responsibilities to achieve each work component.

* You may miss deadlines given frequent re-planning. Even if the project has a perfect plan, but is based on a poor scope definition, it won't deliver what the customer needs. This was exemplified in Figure 2.2. It will be more difficult to identify risks without examining the work involved with different stakeholders.

* You may lose your customer or your credibility.

The list goes on and on. **There are many more reasons why you should have a good definition of the project scope and use the WBS**. If you do a cost-benefit analysis of using the WBS, the benefits compared to the cost or effort associated with creating it are really meaningful and worthwhile. After you're familiar with using the WBS, it'll be easier to create one. There will be a learning curve if you have never used it before, but in a short period of time, you can learn to use it successfully.

CAN YOU APPLY THE WBS TO ANY PROJECT?

The WBS has existed for years and it's presented as a tool that **is good for most projects most of the time**. I dare to say that you can apply the WBS to any project in spite of size or complexity. I provided examples of this already. Additionally, you can find examples of the WBS used in government or large projects, as presented in one of the military standards[1] from the U.S. Department of Defense (DoD) for WBS. DoD uses the WBS in large and complex projects like aircraft and missile systems, space equipment, or sea systems. I've used the WBS successfully in projects **in private and not-for profit organizations as well as in the government**.

The WBS can be used across industries as well. I've used it in the information technology (IT) field and with diverse business projects such as those to create a rehabilitation center, a professional development congress, and a book, to name a few. My customers use it in telecommunications, aviation, construction, and other industries. The WBS helps in construction projects to build a bridge or a building. It helps engineering or manufacturing companies create airplanes, ships, or automobiles. It helps software professionals create software, or people in the telecommunications field who may need to install a mobile system across a country. The WBS also helps with defining and structuring the work of projects related to your personal life. This could include defining the scope of your new house or wedding event, or a two-week trip with your friends. Beyond project managers, other professionals can use the WBS to define their project's scope, for example, they plan to open a new division within an existing company. It helps with defining the scope of research projects too. These are just some examples of the application of a WBS to assist in project scope definition, organization, and communication.

> The WBS tools and concepts that you use across different projects and industries are the same. What changes is the WBS content and the approach you use.

The level of detail that you decide to use in each project in a WBS may vary. I'll discuss this in chapter 6. The WBS also makes sense to be used **in large or complex projects**. In any project, even in small ones, the WBS can help you to manage the project more efficiently and increase your success chances.

---

1   [U.S.] Department of Defense. 1993. *Department of Defense Handbook: Work Breakdown Structures for Defense Material Items*, MIL-STD-881B. Washington, D.C.: Department of Defense.

WHEN DO YOU CREATE AND USE THE WBS?

To create the WBS, you'll need to have the project scope statement, and the WBS must be consistent with it. According to the *PMBOK® Guide*, you'll also need, among others, the requirements documentation[2]. In many cases you can define the WBS and requirements in parallel, and you **progressively refine the WBS** until you create the scope baseline. In chapter 8, I'll discuss further about the project scope baseline and requirements.

The sooner you get to know more about the project work, the sooner you'll produce realiable plans, and the higher the quality of your planning and execution will be. In most of my projects, I start creating the WBS right after receiving the project charter and/or scope statement, or while it's under development. This allows me to start working on preliminary versions to help my team and me to begin gaining a better understanding of the project work.

> **practical tip**
>
> *I advise you to start creating the WBS as soon as possible during the project's early phases. For me, this has been a key success factor.*

As indicated earlier, the WBS is used throughout the project, from its initiation to its closure.

* **Create** it during the project initiation,
* **Refine** it during the project planning,
* **Use** it to monitor and control during the project execution, and
* **Verify** that work from internal and external sources is complete during the project closing.

At the end of the project or while closing a phase, you can use the WBS as a source to conduct post-project or phase-end reviews, to document lessons learned regarding the WBS or project scope, to archive the WBS and scope related project documentation, and to close out procurements.

2   *PMBOK® Guide*—Fifth Edition. 125.

WHO SHOULD CREATE THE WBS?

The project manager is a key person in the WBS development however, other stakeholders must be involved. **The project manager works with the project team, the appropriate stakeholders,** and depending on the project, it might include experts. It's important to create the WBS with the individuals who know more about the work or with those who will be performing it.

> *practical tip*
>
> *The WBS should be created with the input of those performing the work or those with experience performing similar work.*

As a project manager, I've always approached the WBS as an iterative process. My initial WBS draft will receive feedback from key stakeholders and those who have a good understanding of the work needed to successfully achieve the project and go through revisions. In that creation process, the business analyst plays a key role when he or she is available. The program manager and/or PMO manager are also key players in providing guidance and/or helping with the validation of the WBS.

HOW DO YOU CREATE THE WBS?

It's not difficult to create a proper WBS. Many times, those things that help you achieve great results come from simple tools and concepts, like the WBS. Depending on the project size and complexity, it could take from a couple of hours to several days or even longer to develop a WBS. In chapter 6, I provide and explain **proven steps to create an effective WBS** as well as concepts, rules, and examples that will help you in creating it.

HOW SHOULD YOU UPDATE THE WBS?

You can update the WBS at any time before it's approved. Once it's approved, you need to follow the change control process (chapter 8) to update it, and only update it to show approved changes in scope, additions to the scope, or modifications to and deletions of the scope. When you update the WBS, you should review other project documents to ensure consistency.

Similarly, when you update project documents, you may also need to impact the WBS. For example, as a result of a risk strategy, you may need to change the scope to mitigate or transfer a risk. You initially had defined in the WBS to create a product that is very risky to your organization. Later, during risk planning, you decided to outsource the work to mitigate the risk. You need to update the WBS to keep only the first levels of decomposition to this component. You would delete more detailed levels of decomposition because now, you won't create the product. Since a provider will do the work, the provider will decompose the associated work for that deliverable on his or her WBS.

Sometimes, **the WBS is refined based on new information that becomes available**. It can also be refined when it would be clearer to edit or change something. For example, a team member asked me about a piece of work that he understood was in scope, but it wasn't in the WBS. To avoid having the same question and discussion with other team members, I decided to clarify that aspect directly in the WBS by making it explicit through the use of a refined component in the structure.

If you want to **update the WBS to provide further details or clarification**, and those updates don't change the scope, you don't need to follow the formal change control process. You need to update the WBS and make sure that the team agrees on the edits, and then communicate those. This also applies when you need to detail the WBS a bit more. Figure 4.1 shows an example of a refinement of a translation project in its WBS components 1.2.3.1 to 1.2.3.4.

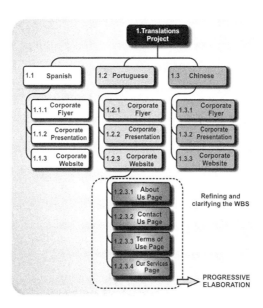

Figure 4.1 Updating the WBS for clarification

In order to clarify the scope of the translations project deliverables associated with the 1.2.3 component, which is the corporate website translations in Portuguese, further details were added by decomposing the corporate website translations into the packages 1.2.3.1 About Us Page, 1.2.3.2 Contact Us Page, 1.2.3.3 Terms of Use Page, and 1.2.3.4 Our Services Page. These are all the Web pages that will be translated into Portuguese and, after they are finished, they will be delivered as part of the translation project.

It's especially important to refine the WBS when you expect to have similar projects in the future. That means that the WBS can serve as a basis or good starting point for the WBS of future projects.

WHAT IS THE PMO'S ROLE IN THE WBS?

Given I've touched on the different factors that can positively influence the creation of the WBS within your projects, I want to conclude this chapter with a note on the role that a PMO can have related to effectively managing the scope and using the WBS. If there's a PMO in your organization, the PMO can have a positive impact in the way you use the WBS and how useful it is. Here are a few examples of how the PMO can assist.

- The PMO can provide training about the WBS so project managers become more effective in its use.
- The PMO staff can coach project managers on how to best use, apply, represent, and communicate the WBS.
- The PMO can create WBS guidelines and templates to guide the process to create and update the WBS and to ensure consistency among different projects.
- The PMO can research what the best software is for the organization to use when creating, updating, and communicating the WBS. It can procure the software and train the project managers and team in its use.
- The PMO can work with project managers to ensure that the WBS is linked to the schedule and other project documents in order to ensure appropriate planning and higher success chances.
- The PMO can ensure that project managers use the appropriate WBS templates and guidelines to facilitate the scope comparison of different projects belonging to the same program or portfolio.

I've provided the answer to several questions that project managers come across while starting to evaluate the use of a WBS. Hopefully, this background information gave you an initial understanding of the WBS and convinced you of its merits.

Next, I'll dive into the core knowledge, guidelines, and tips for mastering your use of the WBS.

chapter 5

What Are the Key Questions to Mastering the WBS?

Sometimes the most powerful tools and concepts are simple. To master the WBS you just need to understand and apply a couple of simple, but effective concepts.

hrougout this book I've shown figures with representations of simple WBSs or portions of them to explain related concepts. In this chapter, I'll analyze the WBS and further explain the concepts, fundamental definitions, and terms that you need to master the WBS. At the end of this chapter, you'll have a very good understanding of what a WBS is, its components, and its main concepts and rules. If you're an intermediate or advanced project manager, you may know some of these concepts already, and you can use this chapter as a refresher, or for new ideas or clarification. I encourage you to read it. Even though you may know some of the concepts, I'll share many different real-world examples and provide a very practical approach.

This chapter constitutes the core knowledge to start mastering the WBS. It addresses the following questions:

- What are the WBS levels, WBS ID, and numbering?
- What is a WBS component and a WBS element?
- What WBS component types exist?
- What is a work package?
- How do you decompose the project work?
  - > When do you stop work decomposition?
- How many components do real-world projects have?
- What are the WBS fields or attributes?
- How do you name a component?
  - > Can you find components with the same name?
- What is the 100% rule?
- What are good and bad WBS examples?
- What Is the WBS dictionary?

Figure 5.1 is a summary representation of key concepts around the WBS. I'll refer to it throughout this chapter.

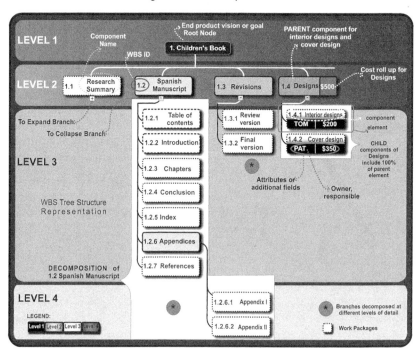

Figure 5.1 Key WBS concepts

WHAT ARE THE WBS LEVELS, WBS ID, AND NUMBERING?

LEVELS

When you start creating the WBS, you identify the work needed. That work is organized at different levels within the structure. Figure 5.1 illustrates that the WBS is composed of different levels that have an associated number as follows:

Level 1 is always the first level in the WBS and only one component belongs to it. In the example, Children's Book is the only component in Level 1. This component is generally the project name. It's where you start defining the project work at a high level. If you use the WBS for a program instead of a project, Level 1 will have the program name. The same applies to portfolio.

Level 2 is the second level; however, it's the first level that you decompose, or divide, with major deliverables or subprojects. In the example, Spanish Manuscript is at the second level. It shows the important components of work needed, and represents a high-level overview of the work structuring. When using the WBS to define the scope of a program instead of a project, it represents the major pieces of work needed for the set of projects involved in the program.

Level 3 continues to decompose, or divide, the work and refines the deliverables from Level 2. In Figure 5.1, Chapters and Cover design are components in Level 3. This figure has a legend indicating a different color used in it per level. Each component has an identification number—also called WBS ID—which is based on the WBS level, or where each component is placed in the WBS structure.

In **Level 4**, 1.2.6.1 and 1.2.6.2 components represent the book appendices. The book will have two appendices to deliver.

Figure 5.1 is a partial WBS so you can't say that you have the total work scope in this case. In order to accomplish the total work scope, you should add the components related to project management and other work.

Each descending level of the WBS represents a more detailed definition of the associated work. For example, Level 2 depicts that if you accomplish the work involved in delivering the Research Summary, Spanish Manuscript, Revisions, and Designs, then you complete the total project scope. The subsequent descending level, which is Level 3, presents the components 1.4.1 Interior designs and 1.4.2 Cover design. These two components further define or refine the scope of 1.4 Designs. This indicates that to accomplish the book designs, you need to accomplish and deliver the design files that will be used for the book cover as well as the graphic designs to be placed inside the book.

The quantity of levels in a WBS—or **WBS depth**—depends on the project. More complex projects may need more detail or more levels at least in some branches of the WBS. This is discussed further later in this chapter when I'll address the decomposition technique.

THE WBS ID AND NUMBERING

As shown in Figure 5.1, each WBS component is identified by a **unique identification number called WBS ID**. These IDs indicate the components hierarchy and there aren't duplicates in a WBS. They represent the level in the structure where each component is placed. After you've defined the work and components in your WBS, you need to assign a unique identification number to each component. This is called the **numbering scheme**.

In general, the WBS ID starts with the number 1 in the first WBS level. Then, as you get into the descending levels, you need to identify each component through the WBS ID of its parent, or overarching, component. Figure 5.2 serves as an example of this.

```
1.  Children's Book
    1.1 Research Summary
    1.2 Spanish Manuscript
        1.2.1 Table of Contents
        1.2.2 Introduction
        1.2.3 ...
        ....
        1.2.6 Appendices
            1.2.6.1 Appendix I
            1.2.6.2 Appendix II
```

In Figure 5.2, the Children's Book component is identified as number 1, and it's the parent of 1.1 Research Summary and 1.2 Spanish Manuscript components, which are its **children**. The 1.2.6 Appendices component also has children which are 1.2.6.1 Appendix I and 1.2.6.2 Appendix II.

Figure 5.2 Numbering the components

Figure 5.3 details component 1.2.6.1 Appendix I from this WBS which indicates what each part of its WBS ID represents.

Figure 5.3 WBS ID representation

To determine what level you're looking at in a component, just count the quantity of characters in its WBS ID. In this example you have four characters (1, 2, 6, and 1) for Appendix I. So you can determine that you are at Level 4.

> **practical tip**
>
> *When projects are part of a program or portfolio, you may need to differentiate them. One common practice is to add a prefix to differentiate such projects.*

If you have two projects (in a program) to create a product for two different departments in the organization, one project for Marketing and another one for Finance, the WBS ID for the marketing product project could start with MKT.1 and the finance product project could start with FIN.1. Then, you will have WBS IDs such as MKT.1.12 or FIN.1.3.2.

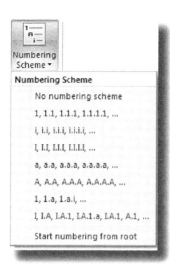

If you use software to create the WBS, some of them provide the ability to **personalize your numbering scheme**. For example, instead of using numbers like 1, 1.1, 1.1.1, or 1.1.2, the software allows you to use letters or other systems like A, B, C, A.1, A.2, and A.3, or I, II, III, and IV. Figure 5.4 shows how MindView® presents the numbering scheme. Chapter 7 presents additional discussion on how to implement the WBS numbering using different software.

Figure 5.4 Numbering scheme

If you're wondering if you should **start your WBS ID numbering with zero or one**, here are a couple of thoughts. First of all, you can define the numbering scheme as you wish. You determine if you'll use numbers, letters, or roman numerals. You also decide if you'll start with zero instead of one if that works for you. Figure 5.5 shows the difference.

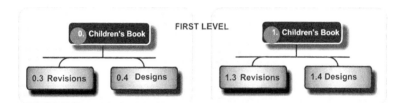

Figure 5.5 First Level of the WBS with WBS ID of 0 or 1

As you can see in Figure 5.5, the left image WBS starts with zero while the right image WBS starts the WBS IDs with one. Either way is acceptable. However, I once started numbering my WBS with zero in a tabular view in a spreadsheet. I had many WBS components and I numbered them all manually. Then, I decided to use software to create the WBS. When I imported the WBS to the software, I realized that the software didn't allow me to start in zero! It required for me to start in one. So I had to assign all the WBS IDs again. For example, in Microsoft® Project, the WBS ID by default starts in one. If you develop a WBS in a spreadsheet numbered 0, 0.1, 0.2, etc. and import that into Microsoft® Project, that won't work unless you use a custom (personalized) filed.

WHAT IS A WBS COMPONENT AND A WBS ELEMENT?

THE COMPONENT

I've mentioned the word component on several occasions in prior chapters and now want to show you exactly what it is. A **WBS component** is *"an entry in the WBS that can be at any level."*[1] In simple terms, you could say that each box in the WBS depicted in Figure 5.5 is called a WBS component. For example, 1.4. Designs is a WBS component, 1.3 Revisions is a component, and 1. Book is also a WBS component. All the components together sum the total project scope. The work package is a particular case of a component. All work packages back in Figure 5.1 are indicated with a dotted line for easy recognition.

THE ELEMENT

The **WBS Element** is *"any single WBS component and its associated WBS attributes contained within an individual WBS."*[2] Each WBS element belongs to only one parent WBS element.

WBS Element = WBS Component + Attributes

From Figure 5.1 at the beginning of this chapter you could say that:

WBS Component = 1.4.1 + Interior Designs
WBS Element = 1.4.1 + Interior Designs + Tom + $200

Tom is the responsible for the deliverable, and $200 is the budget to execute that component.

---

1   *Practice Standard for WBS*—Second Edition. 5. Author bolded certain words in original quote for the purpose of this book.
2   *Practice Standard for WBS*—Second Edition. 5. Author bolded certain words in original quote for the purpose of this book

WHAT TYPES OF WBS COMPONENTS EXIST?

There are two types of WBS components:
1. Level of Effort
2. Discrete

Level of Effort: *"Support-type activity (e.g., seller or customer liaison, project cost accounting, project management, etc.) which does not produce definitive end products."[3]*

A **Discrete[4]** WBS component, on the other hand, is an end product, service, or result that can be directly planned and measured. It's a tangible, definite, separate, distinct deliverable. For example, a book, an application, a house, or a bicycle is a discrete component.

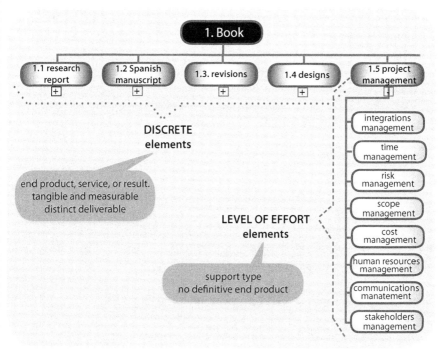

Figure 5.6 Level of Effort and Discrete WBS components

Figure 5.6 shows a representation of a high-level WBS containing one level of effort component, and four discrete components.

---

3   *Practice Standard for WBS*—Second Edition. 5.
4   For a formal definition of a discrete effort, consult the *Practice Standard for WBS*—Second Edition. 5.

This figure shows that **in the same WBS you can have the combination of both types of components** and often you'll need to use both. For instance, in my projects I always have at least one level of effort component I call Project Management. Then I may have several discrete components for the identification of deliverables or subprojects.

You may ask: *"why **Project Management is a level of effort** component and not a discrete one?"* The answer is simple. Project management is not an end result that can be measured or delivered. It could become discrete if you defined the products or deliverables inside this component. Such deliverables could include the project plan, schedule, budget, risk registry, or meeting minutes. Each of these examples has documents or spreadsheets with an end result that can be measured. Project Management is needed in every project. As a result, it should be included in every master WBS at Level 2. Figure 5.6 shows an example of decomposition for a Project Management WBS element.

On the other hand, Research Summary, Spanish Manuscript, Revisions, and Designs are **discrete components**. Why? Because they're end results that can be measured. They're tangible. Research Summary is a deliverable. It's a document with the description, conclusion, and findings of the research before you create a book. The Spanish Manuscript is also tangible and verifiable. It's a document compiling a series of pages contained within the book. Revisions is a deliverable. It's discrete. It's the same manuscript I mentioned, but includes the feedback and input from reviewers. Once it's edited and then approved, it'll become a revised manuscript. Finally, you have the Designs, which are the book's design files. This deliverable can be measured as well. It contains a series of design files like Adobe® Illustrator® with the images, figures, and drawings that will be placed inside the book.

Can you see the difference between discrete and level of effort elements? The differences are easily notable. Just ask yourself: *"can I measure, verify, or deliver this component?"* If your answer yes, then it's a discrete component; otherwise, it's a level of effort component.

WHAT IS A WORK PACKAGE?

WBS components **located at the lowest level in the WBS hierarchy** are called work packages. At the lowest level, you plan for the work, assign the resources responsible for it, develop the estimates, and monitor and control the work. Figure 5.7 represents the work packages with a different color. Work packages are 1.2.1, 1.2.2, 1.2.3, 1.2.4, 1.2.5, 1.2.7, 1.2.6.1, 1.2.6.2, 1.3.1, 1.3.2, 1.4.1, 1.4.2, and 1.4.3. There are also hidden work packages below 1.1.

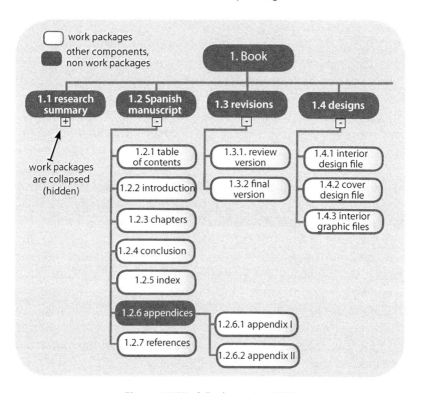

Figure 5.7 Work Packages in a WBS

Why isn't 1.2.6 in the list? Is 1.2.6 (appendices) not a work package? No, 1.2.6 isn't a work package because it's not at the lowest level of the branch, it has two children— 1.2.6.1 appendix I and 1.2.6.2 appendix II.

Work packages should be detailed enough to enable the identification of activities or tasks as well as milestones once you start creating the project schedule (after the scope is defined).

Sometimes there's confusion among the difference between a work package and a task or activity. The difference is explained in chapter 9 when I discuss how the WBS differs from the schedule.

HOW DO YOU DECOMPOSE THE PROJECT WORK?

The **decomposition technique** is used to create a WBS. It's used to structure the WBS and to subdivide the project work and deliverables, to the work package level. Again, it's to divide the work into smaller pieces that you can manage better. It helps to decompose any type of work. You subdivide the work for each of the deliverables into its fundamental components, starting from the first level and working downwards to increasing levels of detail, until the deliverables have enough detail to allow you to manage the work. That means until you are able to estimate time and cost for each work package, as well as monitor its work.

> The decomposition technique is one of the most important techniques to understand and create a useful WBS.

The words "**manage better**" and "**enough detail**" are key terms to guide you in determining the levels and detail needed in the WBS. You'll start determining the best approach for breaking down the major deliverables into smaller ones that you can manage better. For example, if you have a project to deliver several publications and the WBS has an element named Book production, you must ask yourself: *"is that element small enough to be estimated and/or managed, or should I break it down into smaller pieces to understand it and manage it better?"* I believe you need to break it down to better define its scope and you could do it by identifying something like what is depicted in Figure 5.8.

```
1.2 Book Production
    1.2.1 Cover Design File
    1.2.2 Manuscript
           1.2.2.1 Introduction
           1.2.2.2 Chapters
           1.2.2.3 Conclusion
    1.2.3 Revisions
    1.2.4 Formatting and Editions
    1.2.5 Designs
    1.2.6 Reading Proofs
    1.2.7 Printing
```

Figure 5.8 Book Production decomposition

This is an example to show you how the decomposition technique works. It illustrates how you can break down the components to better define the scope, and how you can refine the WBS so it's a valuable input for the project planning, execution, monitoring, controlling, and closing. Figure 5.9 shows the **iterative process** of work subdivision until you define all the work packages so you have a graphical representation of the process flow.

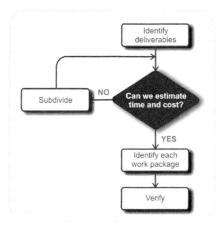

Figure 5.9 Decomposition technique diagram[5]

The book example from Figure 5.1 showed that different components can have different levels of decomposition. For example, 1.2 Spanish Manuscript is decomposed to Level 4, while 1.1 Research Summary is decomposed to Level 2, and 1.3 Revisions and 1.4 Designs are decomposed to Level 3, each one having two children components.

> **practical tip**

To determine if the decomposition is correct, check that the WBS components at the lower levels are sufficiently decomposed and accomplish their corresponding higher-level deliverables.

Different components can have different levels of decomposition.

Based on the *PMBOK® Guide*[6], I created Figure 5.10 to represent the steps needed to go through to decompose the project work.

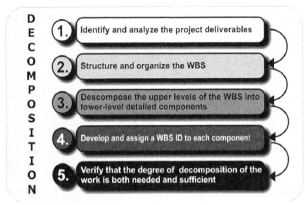

D E C O M P O S I T I O N

1. Identify and analyze the project deliverables
2. Structure and organize the WBS
3. Decompose the upper levels of the WBS into lower-level detailed components
4. Develop and assign a WBS ID to each component
5. Verify that the degree of decomposition of the work is both needed and sufficient

Figure 5.10 Steps for decomposition

WHEN DO YOU STOP DECOMPOSING THE WORK?

There are several rules about when to stop the decomposition. Some of them are based on the number of hours or weeks that it takes to achieve the WBS component. Dr. Harold Kerzner says that *"a typical work package may be 200–300 hours and approximately two weeks in duration."* He also says that *"… a common misconception [is] that the typical dimensions for a work package are approximately 80 hours and less than two weeks to a month."*[7]

This is an example of a rule, however; some project managers don't follow rules. They stop the decomposition when they're able to manage the work packages and to reasonably estimate their cost and time. Based on your project needs, you can decide which approach to take.

> **practical tip**
>
> *Decompose the WBS to the level where you are able to manage and assign the work, and estimate its resources, costs, and time.*

The WBS needs to have balance and to be decomposed only to the levels of detail needed to manage and control the scope. Make sure to decompose it until you have sufficient detail to properly communicate the work. Some projects may need further decomposition and details, while others don't. That depends on factors like project

6   *PMBOK® Guide*— Fifth Edition. 128.
7   Kerzner, H. 2009. *Project Management: A Systems Approach to Planning, Scheduling, and Controlling*—Tenth Edition. New York: John Wiley & Sons. 440-441.

complexity, size, ownership, deadlines, risks, communications, and the organization's resources, culture, and structure, to name a few. Large and/or complex projects generally require a more detailed decomposition than a project that is simple or small. Additional details may be needed when you're working on a project in which you have no experience or domain knowledge.

If you create a deliverable that you need to manage directly, you may need to decompose it to some degree of detail. However, if you outsource a component, probably keeping the decomposition at a high level is sufficient, as you don't know how the provider will manage it and you won't manage it directly.

A very high level WBS is not useful if it doesn't represent the actual scope of work and the major deliverables. That was depicted in Figure 2.2 to show different interpretations of the car scope from stakeholders. On the other hand, a WBS that incorporates **too much detail may not be cost effective**, or may not be the most appropriate use of your time or resources. An excessively detailed WBS could lead to unreasonable costs to control the project. Be aware that isn't always necessary to have a very detailed decomposition.

In most of the projects I've managed, I had at least three levels in the WBS. In my experience with some large or critical components, the WBS had six to eight levels. **A good WBS has at least three levels of decomposition**, especially for projects of an important dimension and complexity. The U.S. Department of Defense recommends three levels in the contractor's WBS[8]. I address that further in the section about WBS and make-or-buy decisions in chapter 10. According to the *Practice Standard for WBS*, the WBS should have at least two levels[9] which I believe is good for small-to-medium projects or components that will be outsourced.

Figure 5.11 shows that you can stop the decomposition at different levels in different branches.

---

8   [U.S.] *Department of Defense Handbook: Work Breakdown Structures for Defense Materiel Items*, MIL-STD-881B. (1993).

9   *Practice Standard for WBS*—Second Edition. 20.

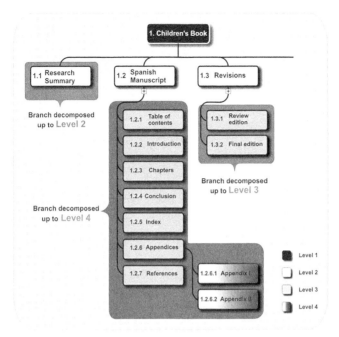

Figure 5.11 WBS branches with differing depth

In order for you to know when you should stop decomposing, you could ask yourself the following questions:

- 🌸 Given this level of decomposition, am I able to assign this component to a person?
- 🌸 Will the team be able to estimate the cost and duration involved?
- 🌸 Will the team be able to determine the activities and milestones from the existing work packages?
- 🌸 Will I be able to monitor and control this work?

If you answer yes to those questions, then stop the decomposition. Otherwise, keep decomposing until you are able to respond yes to all the questions. This is an iterative process.

In some cases, when you begin to create the WBS you don't yet have the information or knowledge to assign a component to a person or to provide estimates for it. This most likely occurs because you're still investigating a certain piece, or because you'll address that component in the future. You must progressively work on the project plan and

decompose those specific component(s) as you can. As the *PMBOK®
Guide* says *"**decomposition may not be possible for a deliverable or
subproject that will be accomplished far into the future**. The project
management team usually waits until the deliverable or subcomponent
is agreed on, so the details of the WBS can be developed. This technique is
sometimes referred to as **rolling wave planning**."*[10]

HOW MANY COMPONENTS ARE IN REAL-WORLD PROJECTS?

While presenting workshops about the WBS, one of the questions
that arises regularly is how many components are in a real-world
project. This is a good question, though it depends on the project
size and complexity as well as on the degree of control needed.

To help answer this, I want to mention the quantity of work packages
I had in two endeavors to give you an idea.

I managed an in-house technology project based on an Internet
implementation which was critical, complex, and risky. It was
something new for most of the team. We had **163 components** in
that WBS. I also managed a series of business projects that belonged
to a program. They weren't complex projects for me to manage, given
I had experience in the area of domain and the projects didn't present
the typical uncertainties and complexities inherent to technology. The
projects had durations of eight months and required a combination
of virtual and on-site management with execution across eight
countries. The WBS for this program had **161 components**. In both
projects, the WBS was created and used successfully. I received
positive feedback about it from key stakeholders. It also provided the
benefits mentioned in chapter 2. These WBSs were especially valuable
in facilitating planning, execution, monitoring, and controlling.

Coincidentally, when I counted the components of both projects,
I realized that they both had almost exactly the same quantity.
Even though the projects were totally different in nature, for
different industries and purposes, and with different teams and
circumstances, it was interesting to note that each WBS had almost the
same quantity of components. The duration of each project—eight
months—was the only similarity between them.

---

10   *PMBOK® Guide*—Fifth Edition. 131.

My conclusions about this are that the WBS is very valuable in projects in any industry, from technology and construction to event planning, mining, and government. The applicable rules and concepts are the same, despite the project characteristics, industry, and region.

Even though the WBS is generally thought of as a single page or a very small structure with 10 to 20 components, in real-world projects, a valuable WBS tends to be more detailed with dozens of components, depending on the project complexity and size. A WBS for projects that span a couple of months typically has close to one hundred components, while larger projects will necessitate a WBS with hundreds of components. I heard that the WBS of the major civil engineering project of Latin America at this point is bigger than the size of one wall.

The number of components presented can't be taken as a metric that serves all projects. However, the examples show that a well-defined and useful WBS takes time and effort to develop and is not a simple drawing you can complete in a few minutes. In the two projects mentioned on the prior page, **the value that the WBS provided exceeded the cost or effort used to create it**. When discussing the details of the WBS, or when to stop decomposing, or how many components it should have, always remember the cost versus the benefit of it, as well as the project dimension.

WHAT ARE THE WBS FIELDS OR ATTRIBUTES?

WBS components have not only a WBS ID and a component name as shown in all the figures throughout this book thus far, but also components can display other information in **fields, or attributes**.

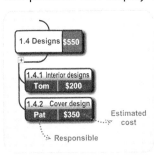

For instance, in the 1.4.2 Cover design component, there is a field for the WBS ID which is 1.4.2. There is a field for the component name which is "Cover design." And you could add other useful information to it, like the estimated duration to achieve the component, the person responsible for it, the cost estimate to produce it, just to name a few.

Figure 5.12 WBS attributes

Figure 5.12 shows a field with Pat as the responsible to achieve the 1.4.2 Cover design component. This field can be called the **owner field**. It also has a field, called cost estimate, showing $350 as the estimated cost to produce the cover design. This example shows the following fields: WBS ID, component name, owner, and cost estimate.

You can use the fields in any way needed for your project. For example, your fields can include WBS ID, component name, duration, owner, and region (for global projects).

WBS FIELD TYPES

There are two types of WBS fields:
1. Mandatory
2. Optional

Mandatory fields are those that always have to be in a WBS component. Examples are WBS ID and component name.
Optional fields are those with additional information that you find useful to add to the WBS. Examples include responsible, cost, control account, region, and priority.

Both field types vary depending on the project.

HOW DO YOU NAME A COMPONENT?

The WBS has deliverables, and thus, only uses nouns and adjectives to name components. This is a core characteristic of any WBS[11]. Since verbs are used to describe actions, tasks, and activities, and the WBS doesn't include any of those things, **verbs don't apply to WBSs**.

> **practical tip**
>
> *WBS component names include nouns and adjectives, not verbs. They could use adjectives if needed. Component names should be consistent throughout the WBS.*

Figure 5.13 uses verbs and is NOT a well-defined WBS. Instead, it's a list of activities with indentation and an ID, but it doesn't fit the WBS definition.

---

11   *Practice Standard for WBS—Second Edition.* 20.

```
1.1 Car Interior
    1.1.1 Install GPS and radio
    1.1.2 Paint interiors
    1.1.3 Install air bag
    1.1.4 Install seats
    1.1.5 Install cloth
1.2 Car Exterior
    1.2.1 Manufacture the frame
```

Figure 5.13 Naming using verbs (NOT an accepted good practice)

Figure 5.14 shows an example of component names using nouns, some with adjectives, and some without adjectives. **This is the way you should name WBS components.**

```
1.2 Training
    1.2.1 Training Plan
    1.2.2 Training Logistics
    1.2.3 Training Delivery
    1.2.4 Training Evaluation
1.3 Documentation
    1.3.1 User Manual
    1.3.2 Administrator Manuals
    1.3.3 Course Materials
```

Figure 5.14 Naming using nouns with adjectives (Recommended)

Whenever possible, try to name each component in such a way that its scope is clear. For example, I saw a WBS to create a car and the first WBS component was named New Car. I would have opted to name it Convertible Car, given the project was going to deliver a convertible car, not an all-terrain vehicle. When you're more specific with names, it helps communicate the scope better. The U.S. Department of Defense Handbook says that *"**generic terms are inappropriate in a WBS**. The WBS elements should clearly indicate the actual system names and nomenclature of the product to avoid semantic confusion."[12]*

For more examples of component names, read the appendices of the *PMI Practice Standard for WBS*, where you'll find WBS examples for different types of projects and industries.

---

12   [U.S.] Department of Defense. 2005. *Department of Defense Handbook. Work Breakdown Structures for Defense Materiel Items*, MIL-STD-881A. Washington D.C.: Department of Defense. 16.

CAN YOU HAVE COMPONENTS WITH THE SAME NAME?

Yes. It's the WBS ID that is unique to each component, not the name.

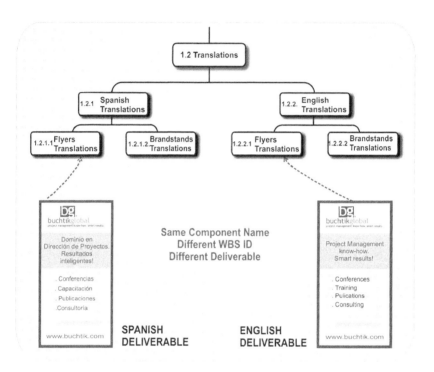

Figure 5.15 The same names for different components

Figure 5.15 shows how you can have two components with the same names but different WBS IDs.

In the example, Flyer translations is the component name for WBS ID 1.2.1.1 and WBS ID 1.2.2.1. However, there is no need to further clarify the name of the components because 1.2.1.1 belongs to 1.2.1 Spanish Translations while the 1.2.2.1 belongs to English Translations. Thus, they are two different deliverables, one in English and one in Spanish. They both have the same name, but different WBS IDs. Some project managers may prefer to avoid using the same component name in more than one component to avoid unnecessary confusion. However, it's still possible to use it.

WHAT IS THE 100% RULE?

The 100% rule is fundamental to create a WBS. The widely known rule, created by Gregory Haugan, *"states that the WBS includes 100% of the work defined by the project scope and captures ALL deliverables in terms of work to be completed including project management."*[13]

Figure 5.16 represents this concept to define one hundred percent of a car puzzle project scope.

> The 100% rule applies to all the WBS levels.

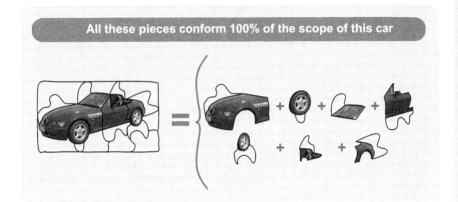

All these pieces conform 100% of the scope of this car

Figure 5.16 100% rule representation

For the purpose of this example, if you have the car's front parts, the windshield, the wheels, the doors, the seats and roof, the fender, and the frame (not visible in the puzzle), then you have one hundred percent of the car puzzle.

A parent component must equal 100% of the work defined for its "child" components. The WBS can only include 100% of the project work, not more or less than that. Based on this, you need to keep verifying if you are following the 100% rule, not only with the first level or project as a whole, but also, in each of the levels. This is very important because I've seen managers applying the 100% rule in the WBS but they don't apply it in each of the levels. Thus the WBS is not complete. To apply the 100% rule correctly, you need to **check for one hundred percent at each level**.

---

13   Haugan, G. 2003. *The Work Breakdown Structure in Government Contracting.* Vienna, VA: Management Concepts. 17.

Figure 5.17 is the WBS of the same car.

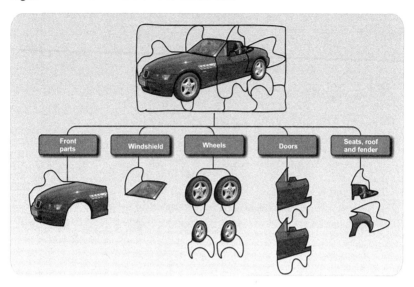

Figure 5.17 Car WBS

You also need to apply the 100% rule to each level, so you'll apply the rule to the wheels scope. How many wheels does the car have? It has four—two in the rear and two in the front. To ensure that you have 100% of the wheels in scope, Figure 5.18 also has to be true and verified.

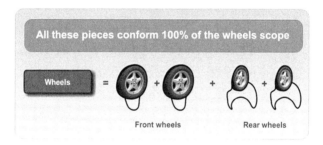

Figure 5.18 100% rule for a child component

This means that if you build two rear wheels and two front wheels, then you have one hundred percent of the wheels scope of the car. You verified that at the wheels component, the decomposition is correct, and one hundred percent of the scope was identified. For a component A, whose children components are a1, a2, and a3, it must be verified that one hundred percent of A scope equals to a1 + a2 + a3 work. This applies to all the components in a WBS.

Once you create the WBS, ask yourself: *"Do I have one hundred percent of the work already represented in the WBS?"* If so, then you don't need to continue developing and refining the WBS. If you haven't captured one hundred percent of the scope, then you need to continue until you have all the scope captured in the WBS.

If you go back to Figure 5.1, you know that you have correctly decomposed component 1.2 Spanish manuscript, because:

> ### Spanish Manuscript =
> Table of Contents + Introduction + Chapters + Conclusion + Appendices + References.

These components compose one hundred percent of the Spanish manuscript scope and nothing is missing.

WHAT ARE GOOD AND BAD WBS EXAMPLES?

To clarify common pitfalls, the WBS presented in Figure 5.13 is a WBS created as an example to show one that isn't developed properly. It's a task oriented WBS instead of being deliverable oriented.

For a WBS to be developed properly, it has to be useful, complete, and easy to understand. It has to be valuable for a real-world project. In the next few pages, I present an example about cars that has proven successful in my workshops where I present *Secrets to Mastering the WBS in Real-World Projects*. This example will help you understand how important a properly developed WBS is in defining the scope and boundaries as well as in managing stakeholder's expectations.

If you develop a WBS for a project to create a car, and by reading the WBS you don't understand what car will be delivered, then the WBS isn't complete or correct. Imagine you give me the WBS from Figure 5.19 to create a car.

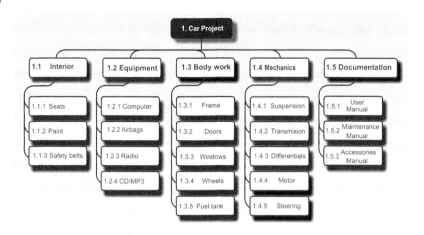

Figure 5.19 Car project (generic) WBS

I'll let you judge if the WBS in Figure 5.19 was properly developed or not, but think about it for a moment and try to picture the car that will be delivered by this project based on this WBS. If I was your customer, you were the project manager, and I asked you couple of questions regarding the scope of this car project, see if you could respond them through this WBS. My questions are as follows:

- How many doors does the car will have?
- Will it be a luxury car or a compact one?
- Will it be a regular car or a parade car?
- Will it have four wheels or three?
- What will be the car's purpose?
- Will it be a modern car or an old classic one?
- Will it be a compact car, mid-size, full size, sports car, convertible, roadster, minivan, sport utility vehicle, or pickup truck?

There are more questions I could ask and you won't be able to respond by using this WBS alone. Therefore, this WBS isn't enough to help you understand the scope of the project and what the project will deliver. What if the customer envisioned a strange car like any of the models shown in Figure 5.20?

Figure 5.20 Examples of strange cars[14]

If you have the opportunity to go to a car parade, you'll be able to see many different kinds of strange cars. You'll realize the variety of cars that different people can envision. I bet that if the customer had envisioned any of the three cars depicted in Figure 5.20 and you planned to deliver a standard four-door sedan, your project would be in trouble. If you had based your project planning and execution on the WBS from Figure 5.19, you wouldn't have delivered what the customer expected.

So let's say we agree that the car won't be a strange one or a parede car. If I ask you what car the project will deliver, I am sure both of us will still have two different cars in our minds. Figure 5.21 shows that I could imagine a convertible BMW, while you could imagine a Fiat car. So still, the car WBS in Figure 5.19 is not enough to help us gain a common understanding of the project scope.

So what is the value of the car WBS in Figure 5.19? The value is limited. It doesn't help you understand the project boundaries or what will be delivered. You can't deliver a roadster when the customer expects a compact car. You can't plan for a $60,000 project budget when your approved budget is $17,000. This is depicted in Figure 5.21. A good WBS helps you to clearly define the scope, like a country map limits defines what is inside the country and what is outside it.; were the country begins and ends. This image also shows that the definition of the scope car has to do with the exterior scope as well as interior scope. Like a country map also define the limits of its states. **A properly-developed WBS sets the boundaries**, it doesn't allow you to underestimate or overestimate the project complexities.

---

14   Fist image of Figure 5.20 accessed from http://www.marjonsplaza.com/funny%20 cat%20car%20strange%20vehicles.jpg, Sep. 2009. Copyright of www.strangeVechicles.com - Second image accessed from http://www.autocult.com.au/img/gallery/full/nickop159.jpg, Sep. 2009. Copyright of PriceOfHisToys.com - Third image accessed from http://showmo-bilesinc.com/images/other/strange%20car_1.jpg Sep. 2009. Copyright of Show Mobiles Inc.

A well defined WBS shows a clear picture of what the scope of the car project is, what is inside the scope, and what is excluded from it.

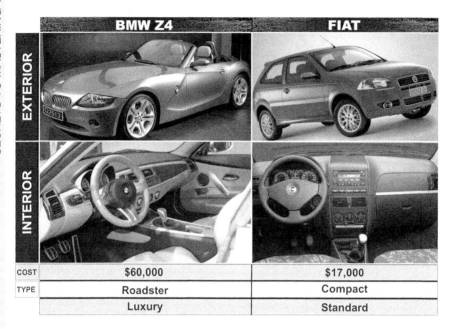

Figure 5.21 Scope of BMW versus Fiat

It's not difficult to check if what you've developed isn't a proper WBS. Just by using Figure 6.1 as a quality checklist, you can verify if you are following the appropriate steps for creating a valuable WBS. In addition, below I summarize **WBS core quality characteristics** as defined by the *PMI Practice Standard for WBS*[15]. If you have these core characteristics it can be said that your WBS has core quality, or it's a proper WBS:

- It's deliverable oriented.
- It defines the project scope.
- It clarifies and communicates the work to all stakeholders.
- It contains one hundred percent of the work.
- It captures all deliverables to be completed, including project management.
- Each level of decomposition contains 100% of the work in the parent level.

---

15   *Practice Standard for WBS*—Second Edition. 20.

- ❋ Its work packages support the identification of the tasks needed to deliver the work packages.
- ❋ It provides a graphical, textual, or tabular breakdown of the project scope.
- ❋ WBS components are named using nouns and adjectives.
- ❋ It's a hierarchical structure of all the deliverables.
- ❋ It has a coding scheme in each component.
- ❋ It has at least two levels with at least one level of decomposition.
- ❋ It's created by those performing the work.
- ❋ It's constructed with stakeholders and expert input.
- ❋ It evolves along with the progressive elaboration of the project scope, until the scope is baselined.
- ❋ It's updated according to the project change control.

By following the steps in chapter 6, you'll create a valuable WBS.

WHAT IS THE WBS DICTIONARY?

*"A **WBS dictionary** is a document that defines and describes the work to be performed in each WBS element. The information provided doesn't need to be lengthy, but it should sufficiently describe the work to be accomplished."* [16]

The WBS dictionary is a document that supports the WBS and further clarifies the WBS content and the project deliverables and boundaries. It can indicate the resources and processes needed to produce each element and it can have a link to additional documents or information about the element. Sometimes the WBS itself isn't enough to provide a deep understanding of the work which is why the WBS dictionary is used. Figure 5.22 shows a section of a WBS dictionary that I used in one of my projects.

The columns in Figure 5.22 may vary according to the project needs, but I always include the WBS ID, the component name, and the element description, at a minimum. Additional columns can be inserted as needed.

---

16   Haugan, G. *The Work Breakdown Structure in Government Contracting.* chapter 2. Author bolded certain words in original quote for the purpose of this book.

Project name

WBS version

WBS Dictionary - XYZ Website Project - Version 4.0

Created by: Jon Turner, PMP | Last update: 4 May, 2009 | Parent WBS: N/A
Status: Approved. | Approver: Lisa Mintei, PgMP

WBS Id	Component Name	Work Description	Responsible
1.4	**Site Documentation**	Supporting documentation for users and administrators of website to be delivered	Tom Palacios
1.4.1	**User and Admin Documentation**	Documentation to allow use and future in-house maintenance of the website	Tom Palacios
1.4.1.1	Online Help for Administrators	Online help that will be available to administrators through the administration panel	Tom Palacios
1.4.1.1.1	Site Administrator how-to instructions	Quick how-to reference guide for website administrators	Tom Palacios
1.4.1.1.2	Site User how-to instructions	Quick how-to reference guide for website users	Tom Palacios
1.4.1.1.3	Online Help for Users	Comprehensive help for users on how to use the website.	Anne Sitz
1.4.2	**Technical Documentation**	Documentation for technical staff on how to maintein, update, and operate the system	Paul Stevens
1.4.2.1	Design and Architecture Manuals	Documentation for database administrators architects, and deelopers to maintain the site	Paul Stevens

Figure 5.22 WBS dictionary example

The key field here is the **work description**. This is the column that clarifies and describes the scope for each element. The component name is not long or detailed enough to allow you to understand the scope. The component description expands on the component name to indicate the statement of work for each element. This helps to eliminate or minimize misunderstandings about scope, or different expectations around what exactly each WBS component means.

> ***practical tip***
>
> *In my experience, when I deal with large or complex projects I need a WBS dictionary to further clarify the WBS and communicate it effectively. If I manage a small or simple project, or something that our project team is familiar with, then I often don't need to develop a WBS dictionary.*

A practical use of the WBS dictionary is to discuss the project scope with the stakeholders and to **manage their expectations**. Given every stakeholder may picture the work in their mind differently; the WBS dictionary **helps to clear up any ambiguities**. The WBS is very clear for those who developed it, but sometimes it's not as clear for those who weren't part of its creation. As a result, the WBS dictionary facilitates the communication of the project work and its boundaries. It also **helps to discuss work assignments** with team members. The dictionary ensures that each element can be clearly communicated. The WBS dictionary may include additional information like key cost and resource information. For communication purposes, you may suppress certain columns when they aren't appropriate for the audience.

The WBS dictionary is part of the scope baseline which will be discussed in chapter 8. However, some project managers who use the WBS don't use the WBS dictionary.

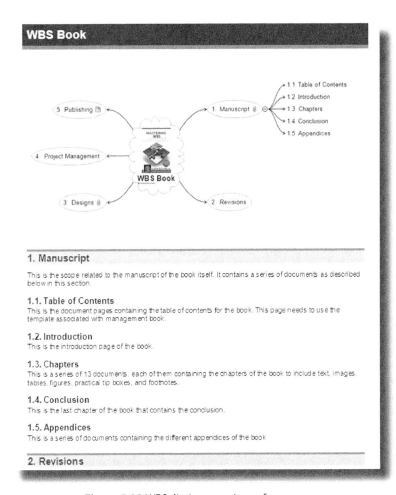

Figure 5.23 WBS dictionary using software

You may ask what the level of effort of creating a WBS dictionary is versus its value. If you create the WBS dictionary after the WBS is finished, the level of effort is minimal. If you created the WBS with a tabular representation, you'll only need to add the element description column in it. The effort is also minimized because when you create a WBS and use software, some software creates the WBS dictionary for you. You just need to enter the description of each element. For example, with MindView®, you can export your WBS to Microsoft Word and it'll create a document with the WBS in a tree and outline format. This is represented in Figure 5.23 using MindView®. This way your WBS dictionary will be created very fast. WBS Chart Pro for example provides a sample file with a WBS dictionary view that can be used as a starting point to create your WBS dictionary. See chapter 7 for more information.

There is no way you can master the WBS if you don't master the fundamentals in this chapter.

This concludes one of the most relevant chapters to understand and start mastering the WBS. The core definitions, rules, and concepts were presented with a rich variety of examples and images to easily incorporate them into your real-world projects.

Now that I've set the stage and provided the necessary core concepts and techniques that you need, you are ready for the next chapter that will show you the steps for creating a valuable WBS. There, I'll guide you through what I call *Bg® Steps to Create a Valuable WBS* which is a series of proven steps that I created and use in real-world projects. I'll explain everything you need to create a properly-developed WBS to ensure scope management success. The next chapter will also present a series of tools, techniques, approaches, and other valuable resources to help you create a valuable WBS.

chapter 6

How Do You Create a Valuable WBS?

You don't need to reinvent the wheel. Just follow the steps needed for the outcome you desire.

*I*n this chapter, I explain the fundamental concepts and steps for creating a WBS with what you need to substantially improve your project scope management. I provide a one-page visual summary of the steps for you to either use it as a guide or as a checklist while creating a WBS. This chapter is of significant importance as it also introduces and discusses the theory behind a properly developed WBS. To accompany the strong ingredient of theory, all the aforementioned steps, either in this chapter or in subsequent ones, are supported by examples of real-world projects. I discuss the following questions and topics:

- ❀ What are the steps to creating a valuable WBS?
- ❀ What are the approaches to creating a WBS?
- ❀ Should you create a high-level or a detailed WBS?
- ❀ What are the options to represent the WBS?
    - > Tree, outline, and tabular representation
    - > Representation types comparison chart
- ❀ What are the tools or techniques to create a WBS?
- ❀ Can you use templates, standards and guidelines?
    - > How do you create and use a WBS template?

...T ARE THE STEPS TO CREATING A VALUABLE WBS?

...organized and use a series of simple steps, the **Bg® Steps to Create a Valuable WBS.** Figure 6.1 illustrates and summarizes each of these steps. I suggest that you use this figure as a key reference when you start creating a WBS.

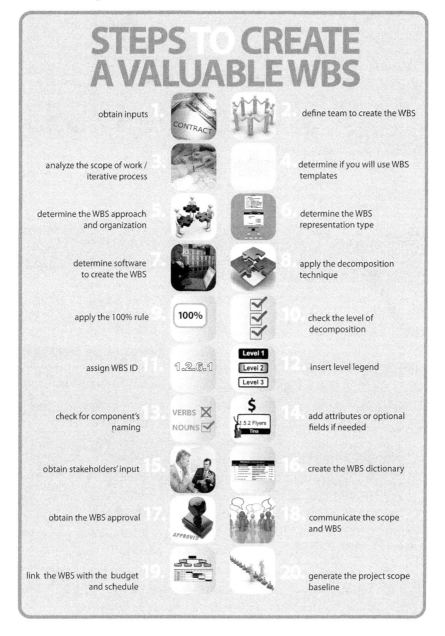

Figure 6.1 Bg® Steps to Create a Valuable WBS

By looking at Figure 6.1, you may feel overwhelmed with the number of steps. The fact that I suggest 20 steps doesn't mean it's a long or difficult process. Many of the steps are simple. You'll quickly learn the steps as you use them. Don't expect to understand every step right now. You'll become familiar with each of them as the discussion progresses.

1: OBTAIN INPUTS

This first step is to obtain the inputs needed to create your WBS, which according to the *PMBOK® Guide*[1] are:

1. The project scope statement
2. The project scope management plan
3. The requirements documentation and
4. The organizational process assets (for example, WBS templates, policies, procedures, project files, and lessons from previous projects) and environmental factors.

This will provide the starting point to create the WBS. I'll discuss more about WBS inputs in chapter 8.

2: DEFINE THE TEAM TO CREATE THE WBS

Determine who will help you to define and verify the WBS. For example, stakeholders, team members, experts, colleagues, your boss, and the project sponsor. This was discussed in chapter 4 when I addressed who should create the WBS.

3: ANALYZE THE SCOPE OF WORK

With the team defined in prior step, start identifying and analyzing the work needed to accomplish the project, and remember that this is an **iterative process**.

4: DETERMINE IF YOU WILL USE WBS TEMPLATES

Determine if you'll use a WBS template as a starting point. You'll learn more about WBS templates in this chapter.

---

1   *PMBOK® Guide*—Fifth Edition. 106.

5: DETERMINE THE WBS APPROACH AND ORGANIZATION

Determine how you'll structure and organize the work. What approach you'll use, for example, oriented to major deliverables, project phases, subprojects, geographic location, functional areas, or other approaches. In this chapter I'll address in detail each of these approaches. You'll see in Figure 6.2 the different approaches that you can select for this step.

6: DETERMINE THE REPRSENTATION TYPE

Determine what representation type you'll use: tree structure, outline, or tabular. You'll see in Figure 6.3 the different types that you can select for this step. I'll address these types on page 84 to 86.

7: DETERMINE SOFTWARE TO CREATE THE WBS

Determine which software tool, if any, you'll use to create, maintain and communicate the WBS. There is a comprehensive discussion in chapter 7 to help you evaluate the most popular software available in the market for the WBS creation and maintenance.

8: APPLY THE DECOMPOSITION TECHNIQUE

Once you've defined the main deliverables, break them down into their components. Decompose the WBS levels into descending levels until you can manage the work. In general, you should have at least three levels of decomposition for a meaningful WBS as discussed in chapter 5.

9: APPLY THE 100% RULE

Apply the 100% rule (page 63) to verify if all the work—and only the work needed—is included in the WBS. Check to make sure that there is no work redundancy or overlapping, meaning that the same work is in more than one component.

10: CHECK THE LEVEL OF DECOMPOSITION

Determine if all the branches and components in the WBS are decomposed to the appropriate level to be able to manage them. Chapter 5 addressed when you should stop decomposing.

11: ASSIGN WBS IDS

practical tip

If you'll assign the WBS IDs manually, do that at the very end, when the WBS is finished or agreed upon. This will limit the amount of rework in updating the numbering.

Assign a WBS ID to each of the components (chapter 5). This is simple if you use software that does this automatically, but it can be tedious if you have to do it manually.

12: INSERT LEVEL LEGEND

Insert a legend of the different WBS levels if you had highlighted or colored each level differently. An example of using legends was depicted in Figure 5.1.

13: CHECK FOR COMPONENT'S NAMING

Check if the naming convention in each components is appropriate and consistent across the WBS (chapter 5). Make sure you used nouns instead of verbs.

14: ADD ATTRIBUTES

Determine if you would like to add optional fields or attributes to the components (chapter 5). I suggest always using the owner field to assign the person accountable for each component. You can do this when creating the WBS or later, during project scheduling, when decomposing the work packages into activities. I suggest doing it, at least at a high level, during the creation of the WBS. The person who is assigned the ownership of a package is ultimately who will work with the project manager in the decomposition of that piece of work.

15: OBTAIN STAKEHOLDER'S INPUT

Discuss the WBS with your project team and stakeholders to start a series of iterations and revisions until you reach an agreement with key stakeholders. Stakeholders may be internal and/or external.

16: CREATE WBS DICTIONARY

Create the WBS dictionary (chapter 5) in parallel with step 15.

17: OBTAIN WBS APPROVAL

Get WBS approval. After the WBS is approved, it'll go through the formal change control process if updates arise. This will be discussed further in chapter 8 under the topics of scope baseline and scope change.

18: COMMUNICATE THE SCOPE

Communicate the WBS and WBS dictionary to appropriate stakeholders to make sure they all understand the scope clearly.

19: LINK THE WBS WITH THE SCHEDULE AND COSTS

This step has proven to be very successful in managing projects, I have dedicated an entire chapter to discuss it thoroughly in chapter 9.

20: GENERATE THE SCOPE BASELINE

With the project scope statement, the WBS, and the WBS dictionary, you can now generate the project scope baseline. From this point forward, if changes to the scope are requested, they should be evaluated against the scope baseline. Further discussion can be found in chapter 8.

Now that you've learned what the steps to use in creating a valuable WBS are, you can refer to Figure 6.1 as a quality checklist when creating your next WBS. Several of the steps just described will continue to be explained in subsequent chapters.

WHAT ARE THE APPROACHES TO CREATING A WBS?

There are several valid ways to structure a WBS and its decomposition (Figure 6.2). No matter which way you group the higher levels of the WBS, the lowest levels are always the same.

I'll discuss the following approaches to structuring the WBS: by major deliverables, by project phases, by subprojects, by geographic location, by responsible unit (division or department), and finally, a combination of different approaches.

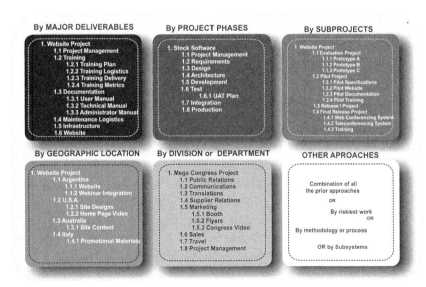

Figure 6.2 Types of common WBS approaches

1.   BY MAJOR DELIVERABLES

You can structure the WBS by major deliverables, and then you start breaking them down. The WBS in the upper left corner of Figure 6.2 shows an example of this approach. Its major deliverables are 1.1 Project management, 1.2 Training, 1.3 Documentation, 1.4 Maintenance logistics, 1.5 Infrastructure, and 1.6 Website. Under those major deliverables you continue to breakdown the project scope as shown for example in 1.3 Documentation, with the 1.3.1 User manual, 1.3.2 Technical manual, and 1.3.3 Administrator manual. This is one of the approaches I use more often.

2.   BY PROJECT PHASE

You can structure the WBS by project life cycle phases. Project phases will be placed at the higher levels in the structure and deliverables in the lower levels. In Figure 6.2, the second WBS in the upper row shows an example of this approach. Using this figure as an example from the information technology field, the Stock software project has the following phases listed at Level 2: 1.1 Project management, 1.2 Requirements, 1.3 Design, 1.4 Architecture, 1.5. Development, 1.6 Test, 1.7 Integration, and 1.8 Production. Depending on the project industry and needs there could be several ways to represent project phases.

3.   BY SUBPROJECTS

You can structure the WBS by subprojects that may be developed internally or externally to the organization. In Figure 6.2, the WBS in the upper right corner shows an example of this approach where your first level of decomposition may include these subprojects: 1.1 Evaluation project, 1.2 Pilot project, 1.3 Release I project, and 1.4 Final release project. Different subprojects are often contracted out to providers external to the organization. If you contracted out the 1.1 Evaluation project, then this subproject requires its own WBS which the provider is responsible for creating as part of the contract. With this approach you'll have subprojects in the higher WBS levels and deliverables in the lower levels.

4.   BY GEOGRAPHIC LOCATION

You can structure the WBS by grouping the work that is achieved in different geographic locations. When you manage virtual or global project teams, you may have specific considerations. In Figure 6.2, the WBS in the lower left corner shows an example of this approach where you may want to group the deliverables by region or country in the higher WBS levels as follows: 1.1 Argentina, 1.2 USA, 1.3 Australia, and 1.4 Italy. This facilitates the coordination and communication of work in this context. It also helps you better manage your geographically dispersed team members, the various languages and time zones, as well as other considerations that I'll discuss in chapter 11.

5.   BY DIVISION OR DEPARTMENT

You can structure the project work by the organizational unit responsible for groups of deliverables. Some people don't recommend using this approach. I recommend it but only when you have deliverables that are clearly assigned mainly and only to a certain division or department in the organization. If this isn't the case, you should avoid using this approach.

In Figure 6.2, the center WBS of the low row shows an example of this approach where the deliverables are organized according to the department responsible for achieving them as follows: 1.1 Public Relations, 1.2 Communication, 1.3 Translations, 1.4 Supplier Relations, 1.5 Marketing, 1.6 Sales, 1.7 Travel, and 1.8 Project management. This represents Level 2 of a WBS for a project I managed. Inside 1.5 Marketing component I listed deliverables like 1.5.1 Booth, 1.5.2 Flyers, 1.5.3 Congress video, and these are all discrete components. **They are all *deliverables* in the lowest levels despite its structuring in the higher levels.** Using this approach, the major portion of the work is generally under a single manager. This makes it easier to assign resources, even though it could be challenging to coordinate across departments. The use of this approach depends on how you have the project team organized.

6.   OTHER APPROACHES

There are other approaches like structuring the WBS by business function, by process, by riskiest work, or by subsystems. Different approaches can also be combined. In addition, you can use certain approaches for some WBS branches and distinct approaches for the rest of the WBS. In larger projects, it's common to see a combination of approaches.

It's up to you to decide how you'll structure your WBS because every project has unique characteristics. Thus, you'll need to consider which approach will work best in your particular scenario. The one approach that I use the most is based on major deliverables, followed by a combination of major deliverables categorized departmentally. I also use the approach by geographic location. I have found that sometimes I start the structuring and decomposition using one approach and it's not too effective, so I decide to change the approach and select a better one for the specific project needs.

SHOULD YOU CREATE A HIGH-LEVEL OR A DETAILED WBS?

I've found that the more detailed the WBS is, the more successful the project. I don't mean that this is the best decision for all the projects all the time, but in the kind of projects I've managed that approach has been very positive.

Having a more detailed WBS doesn't mean to forget the cost-benefit analysis. Make sure that the effort to develop the WBS is consistent with the value it's providing for the project. Below, I present a few benefits of the more detailed approach to share why I use it more often.

BENEFITS OF THE DETAILED APPROACH

PMI *Practice Standard for WBS* recognizes that more detail provides the path for better plans and execution. It says: *"Successful project management relies on thorough planning. This begins by defining the* project objectives with **sufficiently detailed** information. The [WBS] provides the foundation for defining work as it relates to project objectives."[2]

Other benefits of the detailed approach are as follows. A more detailed WBS:

practical tip

If the WBS is too high level, it will be meaningless and won't assist you in setting the boundares of the project or communicating the project scope.

* Helps to gain a deep understanding of the scope early in the project.
* Facilitates work monitoring against the project plans.
* Facilitates work assignment.
* Assists with decisions regarding scope changes.
* Facilitates and unifies a common understanding of the scope among stakeholders.
* Facilitates the implementation of controls.
* Avoids scope issues and disputes.

There is also a phrase in the *Practice Standard for Scheduling* which says: "...too little details means there is insufficient information for the ongoing control of the project."[3]

I agree with this. I've observed that the more information and details are available earlier in the project, the higher the chances are for successful outcomes.

WHAT ARE THE OPTIONS YOU CAN USE TO REPRESENT A WBS?

There are three ways to represent a WBS. You can use any of them and even more than one representation depending on your project needs. Figure 6.3 represents each type. Below I'll discuss each one in detail.

---

2   *Practice Standard for WBS*—Second Edition. 1. Author bolded certain words in original quote for the purpose of this book
3   Project Management Intitute. 2007. *Practice Standard for Scheduling*—Second Edition. 14.

Figure 6.3 WBS representation types

1. TREE STRUCTURE REPRESENTATION

The tree structure is the most commonly used representation to structure and organize the project scope. It's the representation type that I've used in most of the discussions thus far in this book. Figure 5.11 for example is a tree structure, while Figure 5.14 isn't. The tree structure representation is good, especially for project stakeholders who are visually inclined. For me, this type is much clearer than the other ones.

The tree structure is composed of components represented by boxes, and each box is connected to its parent box. The root node (the tree root) is at the top of the structure. It doesn´t have a parent, and it generally consists of the project name or outcome. You begin creating your WBS from the top, decomposing vertically toward the bottom of the tree. There are three variations of the tree structure (Figure 6.4).

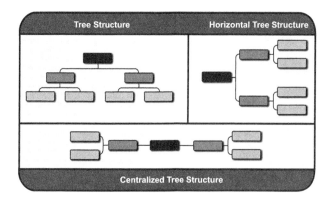

Figure 6.4 WBS tree structure types representation

These variations include: placing the root node at the center of the structure (Centralized), placing the root node at the left of the structure (Horizontal) where the subsequent levels are organized horizontally, or placing the root node at the top center (Tree or Organizational Chart view).

2.   OUTLINE REPRESENTATION

The outline representation lists, in text, the WBS ID and component name for each component. It can optionally display the level of each component (represented by the first column in Table 6.1). Table 6.1 is an example of this representation type.

Bg® Website Project WBS Outline representation		
LEVEL	WBS ID	COMPONENT NAME
1	1	Bg Website Project
2	1.1	Project management
2	1.2	Training
3	1.2.1	Training plan
3	1.2.2	Training processes
3	1.2.3	Training delivery
3	1.2.4	Training dashboard
2	1.3	Documentation
3	1.3.1	User documentation
3	1.3.1.1	User manual
3	1.3.2	Technical documentation
4	1.3.2.1	Administrator manual
2	1.4	System infrastructure
2	1.5	Website modules

Table 6.1 WBS outline representation

The outline type is often created using word processing software like Microsoft® Office Word or Open Office.

When you use this representation type, you can use indentation when listing the components. Table 6.1 shows no indentation. However, Table 6.2 is an example that uses indentation.

If indentation is used, each level is depicted by its indentation. I use this representation type with indentation because it's more intuitive for me.

An advantage of the outline representation is that it tends to use less space in the project documents compared to the tree structure representation. This approach and the tabular one are probably the easiest formats to print the WBS, especially the outline format without indentation.

3.   TABULAR REPRESENTATION

The tabular representation in Table 6.2 is presented through columns in a table. Each column represents a new descending level within the WBS. It's often created by using spreadsheet software like Microsoft® Office Excel. Level 1 is in the left column. The table will have as many columns as there are levels in the WBS.

Each row will have the WBS ID and component name in the column corresponding to its level. As a result, the components are always shown in an indented way.

Bg Website Project WBS - Tabular representation			
LEVEL 1	LEVEL 2	LEVEL 3	LEVEL 4
	1.1 Project management		
	1.2 Training	1.2.1 Training plan	
		1.2.2 Training processes	
		1.2.3 Training delivery	
		1.2.4 Training dashboard	
1. Website	1.3 Documentation	1.3.1 User documentation	1.3.1.1 User manual
		1.3.2 Technical documentation	1.3.2.1 Administrator manual
	1.4 System infrastructure		
	1.5 Website modules		

Table 6.2 WBS tabular representation

The tabular representation in a spreadsheet allows entering a longer, more descriptive component name than those that can be entered in a tree structure. This is because the tree structure restricts the size of the boxes that represent each component. As a result, component names are shorter, and that doesn't provide a precise level of detail for the deliverable scope.

For example, let's say that a component name in a tree structure allows entering forty-five characters while a tabular representation doesn't have size restrictions.

The tabular representation is also useful when the WBS data will be imported from project management software to create other project documents like the schedule or budget.

Figure 6.5 is a section of a real-world business project WBS. It shows three columns and represents Level 1, 2, and 3 . Level 1 is the title of the spreadsheet, this is why it's not listed in a column. It's included in the first row of the spreadsheet, "Congress Project – WBS v1.5." Different columns indicate different branches.

	WBS Level 2	WBS Level 3	Responsible
1	**Congress Project - WBS** v1.5		
2	WBS Level 2	WBS Level 3	Responsible
3	1 Speaking Engagements	1.1 Topics	Tom
4		1.2 Speakers	Tom
5		1.3 Speakers package information	Tom
6		1.4 Sapeakers bios	Abigail
7		1.5 Speakers photos	Abigail
8		1.6 Conference abstracts and presentations	Luis
9		1.7 Congress Program and speakers agenda	Tom
10	2 Marketing Support	2.1 Corporate flyers	Patricia
13		2.2 Corporate video	Tom
16		2.3 Shipping plan	Luis
20		2.4 Promotional items	Abigail
25		2.5 Booth	Brian
28		2.6 Promotion in corporate channels	Tom
33		2.7 Logo	Brian
36		2.8 Congress design templates	Brian
38	3 Public Relations	3.1 Public Relations needs assessment	Tom
39		3.3 Public relations outsourcing	Brian
40	4 Communications	4.1 Communication needs assessment	Tom
41		4.2 Press Releases	Michelle
42		4.3 Call for papers	Abigail
43		4.4 Congress communications	Brian
44		4.6 Congress FAQ	Patricia
45		4.7 Project Repository	Luis
46		4.8 Speakers Template	Luis
47	5 Sponsorship	5.1 Sponsorhsip package template and definitions	Luis
48		5.2 Sponsorhsip package	Tom
49	6 Books Sales	6.1 Books sales strategy	Abigail
50		6.2 Books Quotes	Tom
51		6.3 Books Policies	Ezequiel
52		6.4 Books Pricing	Luis

Figure 6.5 Tabular WBS section for a business project

WBS REPRESENTATION TYPES COMPARISON CHART

Before comparing the three options discussed, I'll first share a few insights regarding how I use these different representation types. I use the tabular and tree structure format only. I generally use the tabular format to create and refine the WBS, and once it's approved, I use the tree structure format for communication, monitoring, and controlling purposes. That is the approach I've found most useful in most of my projects. It's easier to work in a spreadsheet to define the

WBS, and then to modify the text in the columns when necessary. It isn't as simple to add, edit, or delete graphical components in a tree structure, unless you use very friendly software to create WBS.

Another reason to use the tabular representation first is that it can easily be done in a spreadsheet, and stakeholders will typically have the software not only to view it but also to edit it. If I use other tools or software to create the WBS, chances are that not all of the stakeholders will be able to directly edit the WBS to provide feedback (unless they have the same software). Some software providers offer free viewing versions of their tools. This way, stakeholders would be able to view tree structure WBSs, but not modify them.

A final reason to use spreadsheets is that you can easily import them from the scheduling software to create the schedule based on the WBS. Table 6.3 shows a brief comparison among the three options.

	TREE STRUCTURE	OUTLINE	TABULAR
Software needed	WBS Chart Pro™, Mindview®, Microsoft® Visio, etc.	Word processor	Spreadsheet
Speed to create	Depends on the software used	Fast	Very fast
Eye-catching. For visual people	Great	Regular	Regular. Enhanced with the use of colors in the cells
For sales, presentations, kickoff	Great	Regular	Regular
Creation and maintenance	Depends on the software used	Regular	The best. Easiest and fastest, especially for large projects
Scalability	Limited to great depending on the software used	Limited	Great
Component names length	In general with restrictions to short names	Allows for very long names if needed	Allows for very long names if needed
Formatting capabilities	The best, depending on the software used	Limited	Regular
For communications	Great	Regular	Regular to very good depending on formatting
For printing	Easy to difficult depending on the software used	Easy especially if not indented	Easy especially if not indented
To use colors	The best	Not good	Regular
Use of indentation	Doesn't apply	Indented or not	Indented or not
Integration with the WBS dictionary	In general, a separate document is needed. Some software provides it	Yes, by adding additional text to each row	Yes, by adding additional columns to the table

Table 6.3 WBS representation types comparison chart

WHAT ARE THE TOOLS OR TECHNIQUES YOU CAN USE TO CREATE A WBS?

There are several sources to help answer this question. On one hand, the *PMBOK® Guide*[4] presents the decomposition with expert judgment as the only tools to create the WBS. I already discussed the decomposition technique. On the other hand, the *PMI Practice Standard for WBS*[5] has a section that presents additional WBS development tools that can assist while analyzing and defining the work and its decomposition.

Other project managers and I have become comfortable using tools that we learned from various sources. The list below, though not comprehensive, includes the most common tools used.

- WBS software (chapter 7)
- Top-down and bottom-up methods
- Brainstorming
- Expert assistance or judgment
- Mind mapping
- Industry or corporate WBS templates, standards or guidelines

The benefit of using tools like these is that they allow you to reuse portions of the WBS. They provide consistency and repeatability and they help to reduce the creation effort. I'll start by discussing two of the most popular methods used for WBS development.

The top-down and the bottom-up methods are often referred in literature about the WBS. Below, I present a summary of the steps needed to use both methods by following guidance from the *PMI Practice Standard for WBS*.[6]

In the **top-down method**, you start the decomposition of deliverables at the top of the WBS. In other words, you start with the big picture and continue breaking down the work. This is the most frequently used method and the one I prefer most. On the left side of Figure 6.6, you can see the top-down approach represented. You can use this approach easily with the following four steps.

---

4   *PMBOK® Guide*—Fifth Edition. 106.
5   *Practice Standard for WBS*—Second Edition. 17.
6   *Practice Standard for WBS*—Second Edition. 29.

1 Identify the final products, services, or results that the project will deliver. They are the Level 2 components.

2 Define the major deliverables needed to accomplish each of the Level 2 components.

3 Decompose each major deliverable to a level of detail that is appropriate (follow the guides seen on page 55).

4 Review and validate the WBS until it's approved.

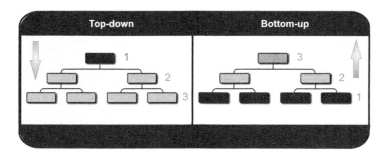

Figure 6.6 Top-down and Bottom-up representation

The **bottom-up method** starts at the lowest level of deliverables—the work packages—and consolidates its work toward the top of the WBS. On the right side of Figure 6.6, you can see the bottom-up approach. Let the following steps guide you through using this approach.

1 Identify all the work packages in the WBS.

2 Logically group related work packages together.

3 Aggregate deliverables to the next higher level, the parent level.

4 Analyze the work again to make sure all of the branch work has been encompassed in the WBS.

5 Repeat until all sub-elements have been aggregated to a single parent, which is Level 1, representing the entire project, and make sure the WBS contains one hundred percent of the work.

6 Review and validate the WBS until it's approved.

Brainstorming is a technique to gather information and to use creativity to generate, identify, and collect ideas and/or solutions among a group of participants. It's not only used for scope management or to work with the WBS but also to identify risks and it can assist with managing other project management areas. In creating the WBS, team members, other stakeholders, and/or experts discuss the project scope and brainstorm the best approach to decomposing the WBS.

Expert judgment can be used for different purposes; however, it also helps in creating the WBS and defining deliverables. Experts bring specialized knowledge, education, and experience to define the scope. Examples of expert assistance could be consultants, business and information analysts, internal or external experts, stakeholders, providers, customers, sponsors, product specialists, a PMO, or associations.

Mind mapping is also a tool that aids in creating a WBS. A mind map is *"a diagram used to represent words, ideas or other items linked to and arranged around a central key word or idea. They are used to generate, visualize, structure, and classify ideas, and as an aid in study, organization, problem solving, decision making, and writing."*[7] The elements of a mind map are arranged according to the importance of the concepts, and are classified into branches to represent connections between the information. Those branches represent tree structures. Mind mapping is a tool that aids in visually representing the WBS, its deliverables, organization, and related information. It also encourages brainstorming. MindView® and MindManager® are examples of mind mapping tools and I will discuss them in chapter 7.

---

7   Online at www.Wikipedia.org. (accessed May 2009)

CAN YOU USE TEMPLATES, STANDARDS AND GUIDELINES TO CREATE A WBS?

WBS TEMPLATES

WBS templates, which are like samples, help you develop a WBS using portions of an existing WBS or a predefined format to create the WBS. They are a good starting point for a WBS especially if a template is available from a similar past project. For example, I managed a project and I knew that the following year I was going to be assigned a very similar project. As a result, I created the WBS in such a way that the subsequent year I would reuse most of it. Further, you can add WBS elements to the template, or remove elements from the template that don't apply to your current project. Some organizations that use WBS templates don't allow for that flexibility or modifying the template (which sometimes is a problem).

> **practical tip**
>
> *WBS templates are especially useful for project managers who are creating their first WBS, or for a type of work in which they have no previous experience.*

Some **software tools come with pre-defined templates for certain industries**. For example, IBM Rational Portfolio Manager[8], which is a portfolio, program, and project management tool, allows for the creation of the WBS, and it comes with WBS templates. The templates can be used for different software project types including small, medium, and enterprise sizes.

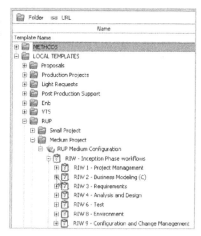

These are templates based on best practices of many years on lessons learned from IBM's projects. Project managers at IBM can use a repository with templates for architectural consulting, development, and other technology-related projects. Figure 6.7 shows an example of an IBM WBS template.

Figure 6.7 Predefined WBS templates in Rational Portfolio Manager

8   More information can be found online at www.ibm.com.

I heard people say that there are also **templates that can be purchased or available through companies or organizations**. For example, the Institute of Electrical and Electronics Engineers (IEEE) created a WBS template for software development a long time ago[9] as shown a section of it in Figure 6.8. When I created my first software development WBS for a project, I looked at that template and used it like a checklist to make sure I wasn't omitting pieces of work that I should have considered. So templates are a way to help identify work that potentially needs to be delivered by the project.

```
                    IEEE 12207 Development Process
                    Work Breakdown Structure (WBS)

1.0 IEEE 12207 Development Process
    1.1 System Requirements Analysis
        1.1.1 System Requirements Specification Development
        1.1.2 System Requirements Evaluation
            1.1.2.1 System Requirements Specification Walk-throughs
            1.1.2.2 System Requirements Specification Inspections
        1.1.3 System Requirements Review
        1.1.4 Functional Baseline Development
    1.2 System Architectural Design
    1.3 Software Requirements Analysis
    1.4 Software Architectural Design
        1.4.1 Software Architecture Description Development
        1.4.2 Software Interface Design Description Development
        1.4.3 Database Design Description Development
        1.4.4 User Documentation Description Development
        1.4.5 Test or Validation Plan Development
```

Figure 6.8 IEEE 12207 WBS template sample section

When I used this template, I typically started with the original template in a spreadsheet, and I read it in its entirety. While reading it, I removed all the pieces of work suggested in the template that didn't apply to my project. Then, I added any work that is required of my project deliverables. That was my first WBS iteration. When I started working with the stakeholders, I didn't refer to the template anymore and refined the WBS in a spreadsheet. When this process was completed, I presented the WBS in a tree structure. That was one good experience I had with existing templates, but to be honest, I don't think is very easy to find or to get existing valuable WBS templates that can truly meet your project needs. Every project is so unique that my advice is that you develop WBS templates tha can serve the types of projects that your organizacion executes, or if you work on similar projects from time to time, that you use past WBSs as a template or starting point to tailor for current projects.

9   Institute of Electrical and Electronics Engineers (IEEE). *IEEE/EIA 12207 Development Process Work Breakdown Structure (WBS).*

I've heard that a WBS template can limit the ability or creativity of a project team during the creation phase. I respectfully disagree with that. **You should only use the template elements that really apply to your project scope**. In this sense, templates become like checklists to help defining work. While presenting about this book in a congress, a project manager from one of the largest oil and gas companies in the world shared this concern. Her organization had WBS templates defined, but project managers didn't have flexibility to tailor them, given their organization needed for all their projects to have a similar WBS structure for comparison purposes. While I understand the need to compare projects, I suggest only using a WBS template when it fits well with the current project and **when it doesn't limit your options**. Remember that the WBS has a direct impact in planning and other aspects of the project, thus, if you are limited through the WBS template, you could be limiting other project options as well.

HOW DO YOU CREATE AND USE A WBS TEMPLATE?

During some of my presentations or training, project managers ask me: *"How can I create in practice a WBS template and how can I use it?"* My answer is: any file that has a WBS could be adjusted or converted as a template for future projects. If you use software, you can save your WBS as a template. Some software come with this functionality. For example, MindView® (Figure 6.9). You just need to save the file as a template and assign it a name. Now the template is ready to be used and tailored—if needed and allowed.

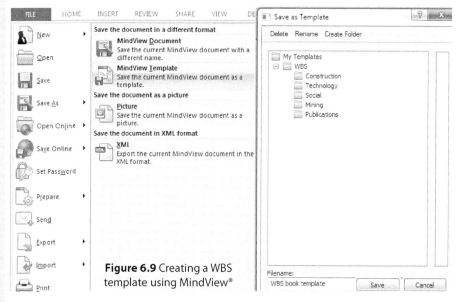

Figure 6.9 Creating a WBS template using MindView®

After you created a template, or if there are WBS templates available in your company, you can use them. Figure 6.10 shows an example of how to start creating a WBS based on an existing template using software.

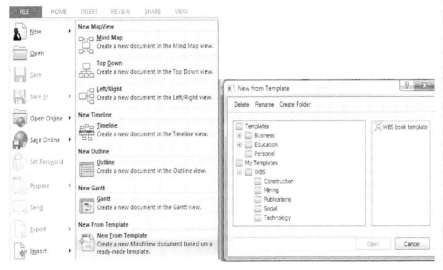

Figure 6.10 Creating a WBS from existing WBS templates

WBS CORPORATE STANDARDS OR GUIDELINES

You can use corporate standards or guidelines to help you create a WBS. A corporate or organizational standard is a *"set of principles for constructing a WBS and might include a format, numbering scheme, naming convention, or required elements"[10]*.

They are often used in organizations that achieved a certain level of project management maturity. When a project or organization doesn't have a WBS corporate standard, this book is a great reference. There are many leading global organizations that have created their processes and best practices related to project scope management and WBS based in this book. One example is *Compañía Minera Antamina S.A.* in Peru, whose project scope definition process based its steps for creating a WBS in the Bg® Steps to Creating a Valuable WBS from page 74.

---

10   *Practice Standard for WBS*—Second Edition. 30.

The standards and guidelines help to ensure consistency across WBSs in the organization. For example, they could present guides like:

- ❋ Color coding can be used to differentiate each WBS level.
- ❋ Each project WBS has to have a tree structure representation

Another example is the *WBS for Defense Materiel Items*[11] military standard used across the U.S. Department of Defense. *"This standard established top-level templates for common defense material items along with associated descriptions (WBS dictionary) for their elements. It includes instructions for preparing WBS, templates for the top three levels of typical systems, and a set of 'common elements' that are applicable to all major systems and subsystems."*[12]

If you've never used WBS templates or standards in your projects, I encourage you to look for some of them and consider its use for your next project. It's not easy sometimes to find templates that are easily adaptable to your projects. Most of the templates I've used are not purchased or taken from other organizations, but created internally to the organization where we execute projects. Those templates are based on past similar projects.

This chapter concludes with the core knowledge and fundamentals to create a valuable WBS. I've presented different tools and approaches to help you make informed decisions regarding how to define and structure the project scope. I've addressed key questions like how detailed a WBS should be and what options you have to represent a WBS.

Now that you have the core understanding of the WBS, you are **ready to get into the next level of mastering the WBS,** which starts in the next chapter with a discussion on different WBS software and how the WBS works and fits into different project management areas. The next chapter will address the software available in the market to help you create and represent a WBS, and chapters 8 to 10 will present how to maximize the value of the WBS in the context of the different project management areas.

---

11   [U.S.] *Department of Defense Handbook. Work Breakdown Structures for Defense Materiel Items*, MIL-STD-881A.

12   Online at www.wikipedia.org. (accessed May 2009)

chapter 7

What Are the Software Tools for the WBS?

In a modern world driven by innovation and technology, we need to know what software is available to become more productive and minimize effort while creating the WBS.

hen I talk about the WBS, I can't avoid talking about software tools that aid in the creation and maintenance of the WBS in fast and efficient ways. As a project manager, you need to make effective use of your time, and shouldn't spend hours manually trying to create or format a WBS clearly and properly so that you can communicate it or print it despite its size.

When I started creating WBSs, I didn't find a list of helpful software. I didn't know where to find WBS-related software, the companies providing them, and what functionalities were available to maximize the value of the WBS through the use of software. I didn't know what applications were the best to easily create an eye-catching and high-quality WBS. I didn't find a comparison among WBS tools either to provide guidance on what options were available related to WBS software. As a result, I thought it would be valuable to review such software as well as discuss how to use them to create and communicate your WBS to the stakeholders. You'll find here the most comprehensive presentation of different software for the WBS and the first comparison chart available in the market about these tools, so you can decide what software would suit your needs best.

"To reach a higher level of maturity… project management software becomes a prerequisite."[1] This was one finding presented in a PriceWaterhouseCoopers report that commented on the use of project management software and its relationship with performance. I believe the same applies to maturity in the use of the WBS. You should use software to create and maintain the WBS and if possible, to integrate it with other areas of the project.

WBS software *"…can significantly reduce the development effort, simplifying the WBS process, and even promoting reusable WBS products."*[2] This is the reason why I review and discuss specific WBS software solutions from different vendors. It isn't my intention to endorse products, I merely want to present some of them that I am aware of or have used for my WBSs. I discuss what I found useful in my experience or based on my comparative analysis. If I didn't present actual tools from different vendors, this book would remain at a theoretical level, which goes against its intent. All the applications that you'll see have many features; however, I'll only focus on those features and functions that are applicable to the WBS.

In this chapter, you'll find reviews for and a comparison chart of seven software tools and two add-ins, and information to research up to 30 software tools. These are not all the tools available in the market, but a good representation to give you an idea of what is available and what the most useful features are. If you're interested in reviewing more tools than those discussed in the chapter, you can take a look at a list of mind mapping software[3]. This online list details a number of proprietary software tools and provides several free software downloads.

I'll discuss the following software tools that are available for creating and maintaining the WBS.

---

1   Evrard and Nieto. *Boosting business performance through program and project management.* 27.
2   *Practice Standard for WBS—Second Edition.* 17.
3   Online at http://en.wikipedia.org/wiki/List_of_mind_mapping_software

1. WBS Chart Pro™
2. MindView®
3. Microsoft® Office Visio and WBS Modeler
4. Spreadsheets
5. MindManager®
6. Microsoft® Office Project and WBS Director
7. Primavera® P6™

I'll also present a WBS software comparison chart and I'll address two additional and related questions that include:

1. How do you customize WBS ID fields instead of using default fields?
2. How do you use different files per WBS level and branch?

WBS CHART PRO™

WBS Chart Pro[4] (Figure 7.1) allows you to create and display your WBSs using a top-down approach. It's provided by Critical Tools, Inc.

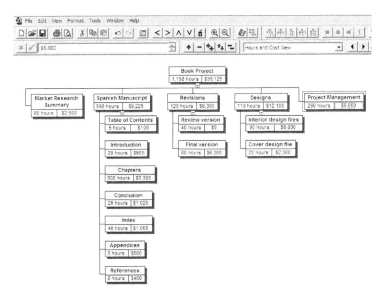

Figure 7.1 WBS in WBS Chart Pro

---

4   For more information visit www.criticaltools.com > "WBS Chart Pro"

This software is simple, practical, with interesting features to simplify the WBS creation and maintenance process. It's fast to learn and simple to install. Below is a list of some of its features.

Add new components. WBS Chart Pro allows you to easily add new components into the WBS. Figure 7.2 shows how to insert components on the left, right, above, or below the component where you are positioned. Note that the terminology used by this tool is "tasks" instead of WBS "elements" or "components" as is the philosophy of this book.

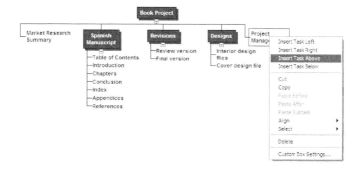

Figure 7.2 Adding components with WBS Chart Pro

Format. You can easily format the colors and text.

Use automatic numbering. There is no need to manually enter the WBS ID for each component, which is time-consuming and has a greater margin for error.

Include a WBS dictionary. It isn't a default view, but the WBS dictionary view in the *"Sample WBS Chart Pro Plan. wbs"* file that comes with the software lists all summary components and components straight down the page with a few fields defined. To include the WBS dictionary view in your default views, you can open the sample file, go to View > Views..., select the "WBS Dictionary View" and click Export. Then you save it to the folder where you installed the software (it should default to this folder where you'll see the other views).

- **Expand/collapse and focus.** Show your WBS at a high or detailed level by expanding (+) or collapsing (-) different branches. Use the focus mode to show or print only certain sections of the WBS depending on your audience. For example, when assigning work to a technical person, you don't need to show the work related to procurement management. Figure 7.3 shows how to focus only in the Spanish Manuscript branch (or sub-tree) and you can do this with one click.

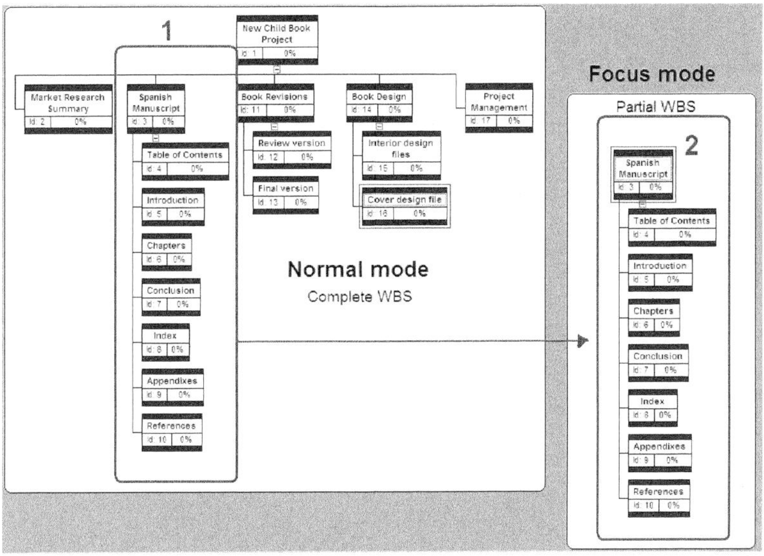

Figure 7.3 Focus mode in WBS Chart Pro

- **Add optional fields.** Add attributes like cost, region or owner. Figure 7.1 shows an example with attributes for cost and duration estimates.
- **Move components.** It's easy to reorganize the WBS and to move its components to different positions.
- **Roll-up estimates.** WBS Chart Pro summarizes the data automatically to each level of the chart. For example, if you have the cost or duration in the work packages, it can be summarized to the higher levels, providing the total cost of the project according to the deliverables estimated, or the total duration for 100 percent of the work.

❀ **Import/export WBS and synchronization.** Transfer the WBS into Microsoft Project or other software. You can also create a WBS from existing data in Microsoft Project. Data updated in Microsoft Project can be directly synchronized with the data in WBS Chart Pro. If you change data in Microsoft Project, with a button click it's also updated in WBS Chart Pro, which is useful to create the schedule after you created the WBS. This is bi-directional, from Microsoft Project to WBS Chart Pro and vice versa.

❀ **Scale printouts.** You can do this to any number of pages. The software automatically increases the size of the WBS to the defined paper size, which is especially good if you want to print with large paper plotters. It automatically adjusts the structure so components won't split between pages.

❀ **Use as a stand-alone tool.** WBS Chart Pro can be used as a stand-alone tool with no other software. This means that you don't need to have Microsoft Project, Microsoft Excel, or other software to use it; it works independently.

❀ **Save as different file types.** Allows you to save the WBS as a Web page or as a picture to use in presentations and documents.

For more information visit www.criticaltools.com > "WBS Chart Pro"

MINDVIEW®

MindView[5] which is a mind mapping tool from MatchWare helps you brainstorm, develop, and structure your ideas visually. You can also use it to create a WBS and then link it with your Gantt chart. It has many other interesting features. Figure 7.4 shows a section of a WBS created with MindView.

This figure shows different features like images, comments and attachments, automatic WBS ID assignment, and components formatting. MindView has the following key characteristics for creating and maintaining the WBS:

---

5   For more information on MindView, visit www.matchware.com.

Figure 7.4 WBS with MindView®

⁂ **Expand/collapse and focus.** You can expand and collapse its components. It has zooming capabilities and it also has a focus mode to concentrate on specific branches.

⁂ **Manage costs.** You can add calculation fields to track project costs and export your cost estimates to Microsoft Excel, which becomes a great starting point to create the project budget.

⁂ **Add fields.** Easily insert attributes like cost, priority, region and person responsible.

⁂ **Create WBS dictionary.** You can export the WBS into a document, and export the WBS index in outline format, which enables you to complete the components description in the document to create the WBS dictionary. One of the strengths of this tool is its powerful integration with Microsoft Office. For example, if you add a WBS component in the exported Word document, and then you import this document into MindView, the inserted component will automatically appear in the mind map or WBS.

⁂ **Export files.** Export your WBS to Microsoft Office applications like Excel or Project, as well as into HTML and other formats.

⁂ **Save as different file types.** You can publish the WBS in a Web page, and save the WBS as a picture.

❀ **Select from different view types.** You can create a WBS in different layout views such as top-down, left-to-right, centered (mind map) layout, outline, and others (Figure 7.5). You can also create a tree structure or tabular representation, and change the color, root, or branch shapes for them.

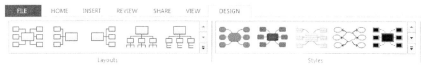

Figure 7.5 WBS views in MindView®

❀ **Format components.** MindView has great formatting capabilities. Figure 7.6 shows the toolbar with different shapes, colors, page backgrounds, and other features available. It has predefined layouts and styles. You can add images or icons to the components as well as select and format several components at the same time. It has several views that can be applied with one click. This is very powerful in terms of the amount of options available for formatting and the ease at which you can apply them.

Figure 7.6 Formatting capabilities of MindView®

❀ **Link with Gantt charts.** Create a Gantt chart or an activity list in MindView from the WBS. If you update the WBS in MindView, the Gantt chart is automatically updated.

❀ **Attach files.** You can attach files like pictures, documents, or spreadsheets to the components. Components 1.1 and 1.3 of Figure 7.4 show the use of attachments.

❀ **Filter components.** Define filters or search criteria to locate and show only the WBS branches that meet the indicated criteria. Branches that don't meet the criteria will be hidden. This could be especially useful in large WBSs.

❀ **Add comments.** Add comments to branches and roots. Component 1.4 of Figure 7.4 shows the use of a comment.

❀ **Legend.** Define legends with different colors per WBS branch. e.g. Manuscript branch is red with a red legend, Revisions branch is in color green with its green legend.

❊ **Create templates.** You can create WBS templates and use them as discussed in chapter 6 (Figure 6.9 and Figure 6.10).

❊ **View for free.** If your stakeholders don't have MindView, they can install a free viewer and still see the WBS you created. They won't be able to edit the WBS with this viewer, though.

❊ **Use automatic numbering**. Select a numbering scheme from a list of several options displayed in Figure 5.4. Starting with version 5 of this software, the WBS ID is correctly assigned starting at the root node, meaning the root is identified as Level 1. The prior version of MindView didn´t offer this.

Figure 7.7 shows some of the different views available in MindView.

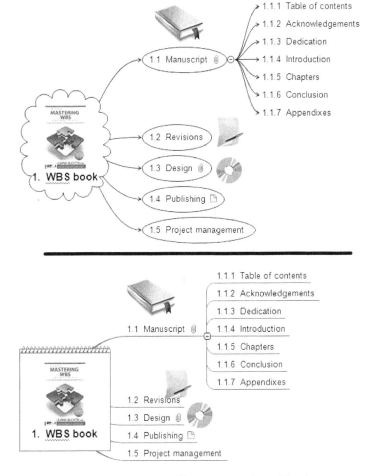

Figure 7.7 Different views of MindView®

MINDMANAGER®

MindManager[6] is a mind mapping software provided by Mindjet LLC. Given I already presented a mind mapping software, I won't detail all the features that can be used in a WBS with MindManager; however, I'll present a brief overview of the tool and an interesting feature for projects, programs, and portfolios.

MindManager has a **multimap view** feature that allows linking different maps; thus, you can link different WBSs. For example, you could link a portfolio WBS with a program WBS and several project WBSs. You can also link different branches or subprojects of the same WBS.

With MindManager, you can create your WBS in outline or tree structure format. You can expand and collapse elements, insert optional fields, use templates, and import and export your WBS to other applications. You can import from Microsoft Project or Microsoft Word, and you can export to Microsoft Project.

Regarding formatting, MindManager allows for clean formatting which enables you to insert bitmaps in the structure, select the style for the overall WBS look, change the fill and text color, or add icons. It allows you to insert comments or additional information through the use of callouts, notes, and floating topics. It also allows inserting attachments and hyperlinks, as well as filtering information.

MICROSOFT® VISIO AND WBS MODELER

Microsoft Office Visio is good for creating WBSs, except that there could be an intensive manual effort involved in creating and maintaining the WBS compared with some of the other tools discussed, especially with large WBS. To minimize this, Microsoft has a free add-in[7] available for Visio, called Microsoft Office Visio 2010 WBS Modeler[8].

---

6   For more information on MindManager®, visit www.mindjet.com.
7   WBS Modeler requires the use of Microsoft Office Project and Microsoft Office Visio 2007 or 2010.
8   http://www.microsoft.com/en-us/download/details.aspx?id=26229 (Accessed in Aug 2, 2013)

This modeler **adds a WBS Template category in Visio with elements to create a WBS**, and adds WBS Modeler as an entry in Visio's main menu. Several of the features available in the other software tools that I discussed aren't available in Microsoft Visio alone. For example, I didn't find a way to show only some sections of the WBS or to expand or collapse a branch. To do that in Visio, you need to edit the WBS and create a new Visio file with a different version of the graphic. However, for those who already have Visio, you can draw the WBS with this add-in. Figure 7.8 shows a WBS created in Visio.

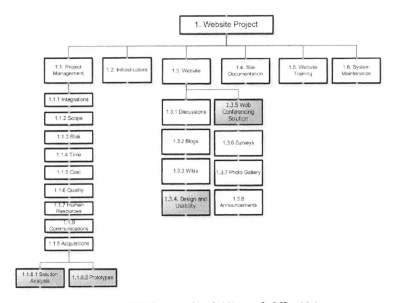

Figure 7.8 WBS created with Microsoft Office Visio

With WBS Modeler, some of these limitations disappear. It allows you to graphically create the WBS in Visio. It uses the Visio functionality and adds features to create and format the WBS faster and easier overcoming some of the challenges of using Microsoft Visio without this add-in. Below, I list some WBS Modeler features:

* **Export a WBS into Microsoft Project.** This helps you speed the scheduling process and you won't need to create the WBS in Microsoft Project again.

❄ **Import plans.** Given that Microsoft Project doesn't have a graphical view of the WBS, WBS Modeler lets you import a plan from Microsoft Project to show it as a WBS tree structure in Visio. When importing, the WBS modeler allows you to draw the entire WBS, or only portions of it.

❄ **Create WBS.** You can create a WBS in Visio from scratch, or from an existing file in Microsoft Project.

❄ **Expand/collapse/hide.** View WBS branches and elements at a high level or in detail with expand and collapse options. It also includes a "hide children" option.

❄ **Insert attributes.** You can easily add WBS information fields like cost estimates or priority.

❄ **Format and add new elements easily.** You can arrange the elements horizontally or vertically, easily add new child or sibling elements, and automatically connect several child elements with their parent.

❄ **Compare a WBS with a project plan.** Compare the WBS structure that you have in Visio with the structure of a schedule or Gantt chart. There is a window that will display the differences between both files or structures. I haven't seen this feature in other WBS-related software. This is especially useful when you receive scope change requests after the WBS was approved and you need to impact the schedule and determine the differences between the existing plan and the new WBS version.

> **practical tip**

WBS Modeler adds great value to Visio in that it decreases manual effort when creating and formatting the WBS.

SPREADSHEETS

You can use any spreadsheet software to create a WBS with a tabular representation, not with a tree structure representation. Examples include Microsoft® Office Excel, and OpenOffice for those who prefer freeware or open-source software. I often start creating a WBS by using a spreadsheet. The reason is that when you start to create the WBS, there is uncertainty about which structure or organization will work best. You go back and forth many times until you have a structure that is suitable. As a result, it's generally easier to change text in a spreadsheet than to modify a tree structure representation. Once I have good progress with the WBS, I export the spreadsheet to create a tree structure representation or I just copy the spreadsheet into other tools. To see an example of a WBS created with spreadsheet software, you can go back to Figure 6.5.

MICROSOFT® PROJECT AND WBS DIRECTOR

Microsoft Office[9] Project can be used to structure a WBS in a tabular representation, not tree structure, by using the Gantt chart view. To obtain a tree structure representation, you can either use WBS Modeler, or there is another add-in that is called WBS Director which is provided by QuantumPM, LLC.

WBS Director[10] provides a graphical interface to build a WBS that is noun-based, and focused on work packages and deliverables. Once the WBS is completed, the activities that make up the schedule are driven from the WBS in Mircosoft Project. Figure 7.9 shows a tree structure representation of the WBS using WBS Director in Microsoft Project.

WBS Director is a great tool if you use Microsoft Project for scheduling. It's easy to install and use, and allows you to have a WBS tree structure representation in the same Gantt chart view. When you install WBS Director, **a new toolbar is added to Microsoft Project** with the functionality that you need to draw the WBS. Below is a list of some of its features.

❀ **WBS dictionary pane view.** As you can see in the right upper corner of Figure 7.9, you can enter the scope statement of each component in the WBS dictionary window pane. After you enter the descriptions for all the components, the WBS dictionary will be automatically created for you. You can export the dictionary into a Word document or print it. The WBS dictionary can be always visible while working on the scope or time management, or you can hide it. This is a very useful feature of this add-in. You can import pictures and diagrams into the dictionary.

---

9   For more information on Microsoft Office products visit www.microsoft.com.
10   For more information on WBS Director visit http://www.quantumpm.com/prod-ucts/project-desktop-add-on/wbs-director/

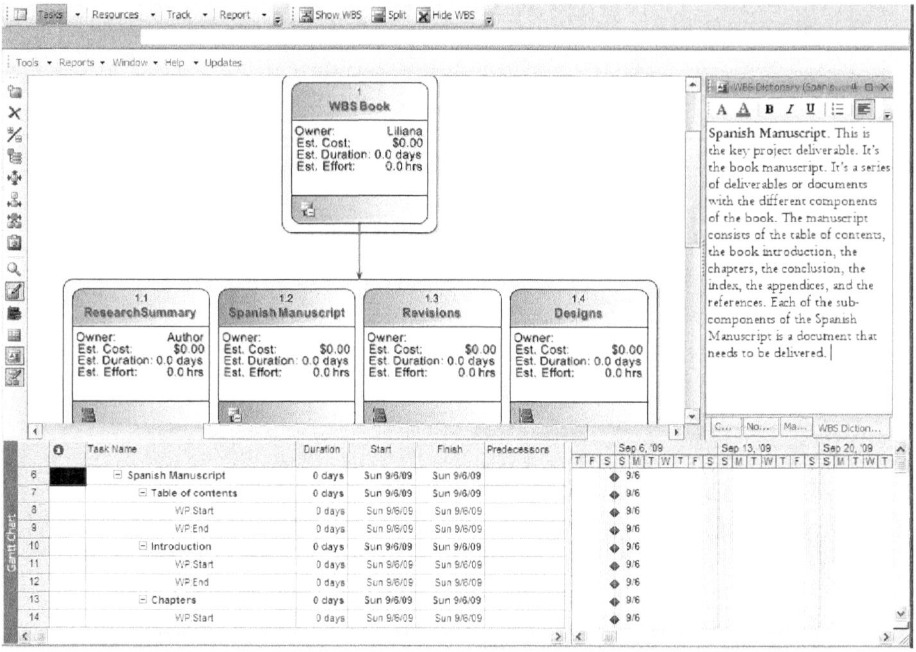

Figure 7.9 WBS created with WBS Director in Microsoft Project

- **Schedule and scope integration.** Manage scope and time in the same interface. Seamless integration and direct synchronization with Microsoft Project. The WBS is created first with WBS Director, and based on its components the activities are automatically created in the Gantt chart. Dynamically change the schedule through manipulation of the WBS deliverables.
- **Spreadsheet entry.** You can either add components to the WBS graphically creating new nodes, or you can use the spreadsheet entry to type the WBS components faster in a table while WBS Director draws them in the graphical tree structure. Through this spreadsheet you can also enter values to attributes.
- **Add attributes.** You can add fully customizable element attributes and properties like name, ID, owner, cost, and effort. You can also check and uncheck properties as needed to identify which attributes you want visible in the WBS.
- **Estimate costs.** You can capture the project costs and budget at the work package level.

❋ **Export.** You can export the WBS to HTML files as well as copy the view to the clipboard to use it in other documents.

❋ **Expand/collapse/hide.** Through the toggle children expansion feature, you can show and hide WBS branches.

❋ **Toggle list mode**. Toggles whether the selected node's children should be displayed in a vertical list. Allows to show a branch in the form of boxes with their attributes, or just to show it as a list of component names that uses less space in the structure.

If you want to use Microsoft Project to create your WBS in a tabular format within the Gantt chart view, and you don't use add-ins such as WBS Modeler or WBS Director, you can use the Task Name column from the Gantt chart view to represent the WBS component name, and insert a column to represent the WBS ID. It isn't the intent of this book to provide instructions on how to specifically use each feature of each software, but given that Microsoft Project is one of the most used project management software, I present below the simple steps in Microsoft Project **to add a default WBS ID column in the tabular view of a Gantt chart**: 1) go to the "View" menu, and select "Gantt Chart"; 2) Insert the WBS ID column. (Go to the "Insert" menu and select "Column…") 2.1) Once in the 'Column Definition' dialog box, in the "Field Name" select "WBS" from the drop down list. 2.2) In the "Title" field type "WBS ID", finally click OK.

> ***practical tip***

Note that it's confusing to use the Task Name column as a way to create the WBS because the WBS is not a list of tasks. As you type elements, the WBS ID column will be automatically populated based on the indentation that you use in the tasks.

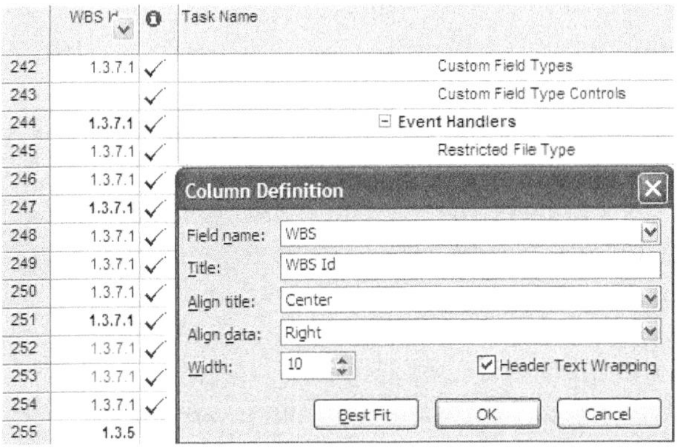

Figure 7.10 Inserting the WBS column in a Gantt chart

PRIMAVERA® P6™ ENTERPRISE PPM

Oracle's Primavera[11] P6 Enterprise Project Portfolio Management is a robust solution for managing projects, programs and portfolios. Originally used to manage large projects or those in the construction field, today it goes beyond construction, and is popular in different industries. Primavera P6 is advanced and thorough related to the use of the WBS. A tabular view of a WBS in Primavera P6 is shown in Figure 7.11. Primavera can be used to manage large projects and a multitude of small projects under the same program or portfolio.

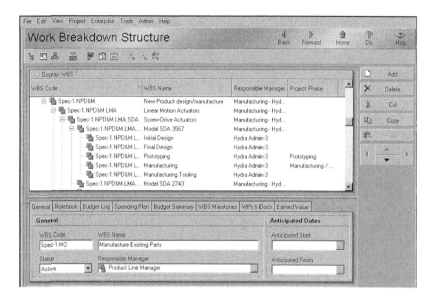

Figure 7.11 Tabular view of a WBS in Primavera P6[12]

Figure 7.11 shows the WBS Code, which is the same as the WBS ID. You can also see the WBS Name which is synonymous with the WBS component name. The Responsible Manager field represents the person assigned to each deliverable, while Project phase is an optional field in this software's version of the WBS. The General tab at the bottom of Figure 7.11 shows how to assign a specific person to a WBS component. For example, the Product Line Manager is responsible for the Manufacture Existing Parts element.

---

11   For more information on Primavera P6 visit www.oracle.com.
12   Figure from *Primavera® P6™ Project Management Reference Manual*. Version 7.0. Page 119. Copyright of Oracle Corporation.

There are several WBS-related things you can do in Primavera P6; however, one of its strengths is its integration with time management, cost management and especially with earned value management. Below there is a list of other things you can do with this software.

Create WBS automatically. When you create a project, the software automatically creates a WBS. No project can exist without a WBS!

Assign category values. Project management, design and engineering, prototyping, and manufacturing or production are examples of categories that you can assign to each WBS element. Once you assigned the categories, you can group, sort, and filter WBS components based on those values. These categories behave as additional fields to provide further information about the elements.

Show work assignments. For each of the components in the WBS, you can show work assignments according to the Organizational Breakdown Structure (OBS). Indicate the responsible manager and map that to the OBS. You can visualize the WBS grouped by components assigned to a specific entry or individual in the OBS.

Summarize information. You can summarize information to a specific level when calculating and maintaining data.

Select from different view types. Chose between views like tree structure and tabular.

Expand/collapse and focus. View an entire WBS or focus the view to a section for a specific node or elements.

Manage programs. Organize multiple projects that use the same WBS by grouping their identical WBS levels to manage your programs.

Integrate the schedule. Through milestones associated with the WBS, you can easily integrate the scope with the schedule. You can also see how the different activities corresponding to a work package have the same WBS ID (the work package WBS ID).

Use templates. You can also use templates to create the WBS from scratch or by copying an existing (total or partial) WBS from past projects.

WBS SOFTWARE COMPARISON CHART

As a summary of the prior discussions, Table 7.1 presents a high-level comparison among some of the software reviewed.

Software For WBS - COMPARISON CHART						
	WBS Chart Pro™	MS Office Visio and WBS Modeler	Spreadsheet Software	MindView®	MS Project and WBS Director	Primavera®
Summary components. Roll up estimates	Yes	Not in Visio. Yes with WBS Modeler	No. Done manually but time consuming	Yes	Yes	Yes
Expand and collapse	Yes	Not in Visio. Yes with WBS Modeler	No. Done manually by hiding or showing	Yes	Yes	Yes
WBS ID automatic assignment	Yes	Not in Visio. Yes with WBS Modeler	No	Yes	Yes	No
Can control default WBS ID	Not with default field. Custom field needed	No	Yes	No	Not with default field. Custom field needed	No
Attributes	Yes Unlimited	No. Can be done manually	Yes	Yes	Yes	Yes
Printing	Optimum Scale printing	Manually	Manually	Optimum	Yes	Manually
Focus mode	Yes	No. Separate drawing needed	No	Yes	Yes with add-ins	Yes
Formats available	Tree WBS dictionary	Tree	Tabular	Tree Tabular Outline	Tabular Tree with add-ins	Tabular Tree
Formatting	Good	Very good	Very good	Optimum	Limited. Expanded with add-ins	Limited
Import and export		Exports from MS Project to Visio. Enhanced with WBS Modeler		To MS Office, MS Project, MS Excel, HTML, other formats	Yes with add-ins	Yes
Automatic element's repositioning when moving them	Yes	Not in Visio. Yes with WBS Modeler	No	Yes. Manual and auto layout	Yes with add-ins	
Direct synchronization with schedule	Yes. Bi-directional with Ms Project	No	No	With MindView Gantt chart view	Yes with add-ins	Yes with Primavera schedule

Table 7.1 bg® Comparison chart of WBS software

Some of the software have limited capabilities or implement concepts that are not aligned with best practices or with the approach recommended in this book. Some are still based on the task-oriented approach rather than the deliverable-oriented approach. Other software tools work very well. If budget is a concern, free software like Free Mind[13] is available for WBS creation.

Something else to consider is the difference between software tools that only or mostly help create the WBS and those that provide robust features to manage most of the project's aspects. When you use robust project management software, you can integrate several aspects of a project like the schedule, budget, risks, earned value, or resource management. On the other hand, some robust project management software doesn't have capabilities to create a high-quality WBS or its approach is task oriented. As a result, you may decide to use specific software for WBS creation and different software to manage the rest of the project aspects. Ideally, it would be nice to use the same software for everything but this isn't always a possibility.

There are a variety of software tools available that are very useful in helping to create and manage a high-quality WBS with low effort.

> **practical tip**

I don't suggest using scheduling software to create the WBS unless it allows you to properly represent the WBS components without confusing them with tasks. Use the WBS ID in a schedule to link the schedule with the WBS, but avoid using a Gantt chart to represent the WBS.

We have concluded the software review and comparison; however, the next two sections of this chapter will present two different and important topics to address when dealing with WBS-related software. First, I'll explain how to customize the WBS ID field when the software is not behaving as you need it. Second, I'll discuss how to manage the different WBS branches in separate files if your software doesn't allow you to have the complete WBS in a single file. These discussions will help you with some common challenges that you may face depending on the software that you use.

> **practical tip**

When choosing software, consider a tool that allows implementing the principles and concepts of a well-defined or high-quality WBS.

---

13   More information at www.freemind.sourceforge.net.

HOW DO YOU CUSTOMIZE WBS ID FIELDS INSTEAD OF USING DEFAULT FIELDS?

When you use the WBS ID in certain scheduling software, the software will automatically assign the WBS ID and then you can't change the way the components were numbered. There may be cases that you agree with the numbering the software suggests, and other occasions when you would prefer the assignment of WBS IDs was executed differently. For example, the software assigns WBS ID to tasks, and you don't need for the tasks to have a WBS ID. In that instance, you may want to use **custom fields**. That way, you won't have restrictions on how the numbering behaves. However, you may want to modify the behavior of default WBS IDs through the use of custom fields. I'll explain this.

1 House Readiness Project
   1.1 Equipments
   1.2 Furniture
      1.2.1 Kitchen furniture
      1.2.2 Bedroom furniture
      1.2.3 Bathroom furniture
   1.3 ......

Figure 7.12 WBS section for a house project

Figure 7.12 shows work packages in the WBS. You need to define how the team will execute the job and the tasks needed to accomplish each deliverable. As tasks aren't part of a WBS, tasks will be defined in the schedule. However, tasks won't have a new WBS ID. **You need WBS IDs only for the components that appear in the WBS.**

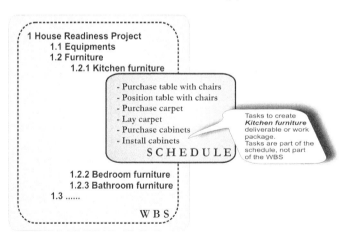

Figure 7.13 WBS section for a house project and tasks

Figure 7.13 shows the tasks associated with the 1.2.1 Kitchen Furniture deliverable. The **tasks are located one level below the work package level** in the schedule. Using Microsoft Project as an example, if you assign the WBS ID in the schedule, by default it will assign a WBS ID to all the tasks under 1.2.1 Kitchen Furniture. It'll assign a WBS ID for 1.2.1.1, 1.2.1.2, 1.2.1.3, 1.2.1.4, 1.2.1.5, and 1.2.1.6 (all the activities), as shown in Figure 7.14, and this is NOT what you need. The "WBS" default field is used for this (first column).

	WBS		Task Name	Duration	Start	Finish
1	1		⊟ House Readiness Project	21 days	Mon 7/13/09	Mon 8/10/09
2	1.1		Equipments	7 days	Mon 7/13/09	Tue 7/21/09
3	1.2		⊟ Furniture	14 days	Wed 7/22/09	Mon 8/10/09
4	1.2.1		⊟ Kitchen furniture	7 days	Wed 7/22/09	Thu 7/30/09
5	1.2.1.1		Purchase Table with chairs	0.5 days	Wed 7/22/09	Wed 7/22/09
6	1.2.1.2		Locate Table with chairs	0.5 days	Wed 7/22/09	Wed 7/22/09
7	1.2.1.3		Purchase carpet	0.5 days	Thu 7/23/09	Thu 7/23/09
8	1.2.1.4		Lay carpet	0.5 days	Thu 7/23/09	Thu 7/23/09
9	1.2.1.5		Purchase cabinets	3 days	Fri 7/24/09	Tue 7/28/09
10	1.2.1.6		Install cabinets	2 days	Wed 7/29/09	Thu 7/30/09

Figure 7.14 WBS section for a house with software's automatic WBS ID

To solve this, in a Gantt chart you can use a personalized text field instead of the "WBS" column that comes with the software. Add a new text column and name it "Custom WBS ID". Then just leave the tasks inside 1.2.1 without a WBS ID, as seen in Figure 7.15.

	Custom WBS Id		Task Name	Duration	Start	Finish
1	1		⊟ House Readiness Project	21 days	Mon 7/13/09	Mon 8/10/09
2	1.1		Equipments	7 days	Mon 7/13/09	Tue 7/21/09
3	1.2		⊟ Furniture	14 days	Wed 7/22/09	Mon 8/10/09
4	1.2.1		⊟ Kitchen furniture	7 days	Wed 7/22/09	Thu 7/30/09
5			Purchase Table with chairs	0.5 days	Wed 7/22/09	Wed 7/22/09
6			Locate Table with chairs	0.5 days	Wed 7/22/09	Wed 7/22/09
7			Purchase carpet	0.5 days	Thu 7/23/09	Thu 7/23/09
8			Lay carpet	0.5 days	Thu 7/23/09	Thu 7/23/09
9			Purchase cabinets	3 days	Fri 7/24/09	Tue 7/28/09
10			Install cabinets	2 days	Wed 7/29/09	Thu 7/30/09
11	1.2.2		Dinning room furniture	4 days	Fri 7/31/09	Wed 8/5/09

Figure 7.15 WBS section with custom WBS ID field

In this second example, the system does NOT assign the WBS ID automatically. You do it manually without using the WBS default field, and creating the "Custom WBS ID" field. The tasks don't display a WBS ID as they aren't part of the WBS. This now is a correct WBS representation in a Gantt chart because tasks don't need a WBS ID.

Another valid option if you don't want to leave the WBS ID column blank for tasks is to **enter the WBS ID of the task's associated deliverable**. In Figure 7.15, tasks five to ten correspond to the 1.2.1 deliverable, thus they should display WBS ID 1.2.1 if you did that.

I indicated earlier how to add a default WBS ID field, now I will go over **how to add a WBS ID custom field** in Microsoft Project. Go to the *Insert > Column* menu, and in the *Column Definition* Window, in the *Field Name* list box, select "Text 1" or any text field and in the *Title* field assign any title or "Custom WBS ID" as shown in Figure 7.15. Depending on the software version you use, this may appear a little different.

The way you represent work in the WBS doesn't reflect sequencing among WBS components or a network of deliverables. When you assign a WBS ID in the WBS you aren't considering in which sequence the work will be performed. However, when you import the WBS into scheduling software, the software assumes that the deliverables imported will be performed in sequence.

> *practical tip*
>
> *Having control of the WBS ID allows you to determine how you want to display the WBS ID in a Gantt chart.*

As a result, the software assigns an automatic WBS ID in such a sequence or order that may not be consistent with the way you want to structure the tasks and deliverables in the schedule. A personalized field for the WBS ID can solve this and enable you to freely control the WBS ID in the schedule.

It's good to note that you can personalize the WBS fields by instructing the system to use other numbering schemes that are character instead of numeric as discussed in chapter 5.

HOW DO YOU USE DIFFERENT FILES FOR WBS LEVELS AND BRANCHES?

Sometimes when you draw a WBS in a software tool that isn't specific to WBS, and the WBS exceeds one page, you may need to split the WBS representation into different files (different pages or branches). For example, if you use Microsoft Visio and the WBS doesn't fit one page, you can create one Visio file per branch. Figure 7.16 shows that a Website WBS has five Visio (*.vsd) files. One of those files shows the highest level of the WBS, which is Level 1 and 2 ("Website WBS – Full Scope v4.0.vsd"). Another file shows the branch corresponding to the documentation scope ("Website WBS – IT Documentation v3.2.vsd"), and separate files show the branches corresponding to the scope of infrastructure, acquisitions, and software development.

Name ▲	Size	Type	Date Modified
Website WBS - Full Scope v4.0.vsd	84 KB	VSD File	6/25/2009 6:13 PM
Website WBS - IT Documentation v3.2.vsd	57 KB	VSD File	6/25/2009 6:15 PM
Website WBS - IT Infrastructure v3.2.vsd	60 KB	VSD File	6/25/2009 6:16 PM
Website WBS - IT PM - Acquisitions Mgmt v4.0.vsd	67 KB	VSD File	6/25/2009 6:16 PM
Website WBS - IT Software v4.0.vsd	81 KB	VSD File	6/25/2009 6:19 PM

Figure 7.16 WBS split in multiple files

This is a simple way to make sure the drawings that you have can be viewed and printed easily. You can only use certain files when talking with different stakeholder groups. For example, if you have a discussion with the executives, you can only show the first file which has Level 1 and 2 of the WBS.

The top right section of Figure 7.17 shows the WBS file containing the entire project scope. This is the level that you typically show to those that only need a high-level overview of the work. There are also three files with sections of the highest levels like documentation (top left section), infrastructure (bottom left section), and software (bottom right section). The file specific to documentation for example will be the one you focus on when talking and assigning work to the writers.

Depending on who you need to discuss with or present the files to, you'll decide if you print and/or communicate all the files or just the highest levels.

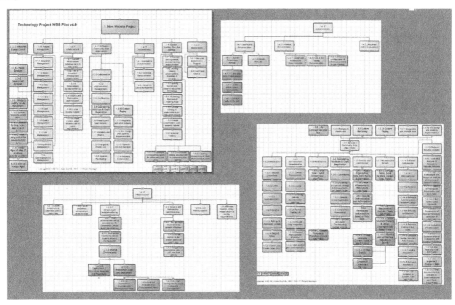

Figure 7.17 View of WBS split in multiple files

I've concluded one of the most practical chapters in this book. Now you are able to make an informed decision regarding which software best fits your need to create, maintain, and communicate the WBS. You also have a good understanding of how to overcome some common issues regarding WBS ID assignments in software, as well as how you can use different files for branches in a WBS when you have certain limitations in your software. Some of the software mentioned is free or low cost. I encourage you to start using WBS-related software if you have not already to simplify the way you work.

In the next chapter, you'll learn about the integration between the WBS and scope management, as well as important things to enhance your scope management practices.

chapter 8

How Do You Integrate the WBS with Scope Management?

It's almost all about scope and how to better manage it. The scope is the basis for planning. Most of our discussions with the customer end up being around scope changes, scope expectations, requirements and such.

ll prior chapters discussed the WBS and project scope because the two go hand in hand. However, there are some additional scope-related concepts that you need to know. This chapter is fundamental for you to continue to increase your knowledge of core topics regarding improving scope management. New topics will arise regarding not only project scope but also product scope and requirements. I'll present how the WBS and scope management correlate with the *PMBOK® Guide* and I'll demonstrate how the WBS positively impacts and influences the project planning. **New material in this chapter includes how the project manager must manage the scope baseline and what the relationship of it with scope changes is.**

You can expect to learn more about the following topics:

- What is the product scope, project scope, and the product WBS?
- What's the role of the WBS to the scope baseline and scope change control?
- How do project requirements affect the WBS?
- What is out of scope?
- How does the WBS fit in with the *PMBOK® Guide*?

WHAT IS THE PRODUCT SCOPE, PROJECT SCOPE, AND THE PRODUCT WBS?

The term scope in the project context can refer to[1]:

- **Product scope**: the features and functions that characterize a product, service or result; and
- **Project scope**: the work performed to deliver a product, service, or result with the specified features and functions. Sometimes this is viewed as including product scope.

This book is mainly focused on the project scope rather than the product scope. The project scope goes beyond the product scope. For example, you have a project to create a website for a company and Figure 8.1 depicts the project and product WBS for this project.

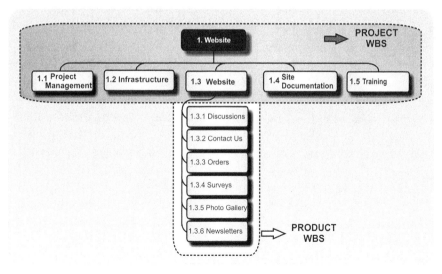

Figure 8.1 Project WBS with product WBS

---

1   *PMBOK® Guide*—Fifth Edition. 105.

The **project scope** is not only to create the website, but also to execute the work related to managing the project such as acquisitions, quality, risks, human resources, costs, time, and communications. It's concerned with the website infrastructure, the documentation, training materials, and associated business processes. Even though isn't listed in Figure 8.1, marketing and promotion of the website launch, website content, and other deliverables are aspects of the project that will have to be defined and planned.

The **product scope**, in this example, is concerned with the website features, functions, and functionality. The concerns related to the product scope include a customer newsletter, order tracking, a photo gallery of corporate events, and surveys, to name a few. In such a project, **the project scope is managed by the project manager and the product scope is often managed by the system analyst, business analyst, or technical leader**, depending on the organization's resources and structure, as well as depending on the industry. Both project scope and product scope have to be properly integrated. As a result, the project manager and the person responsible for the product scope need to work very close together.

The *PMBOK® Guide* says that the *"completion of the project scope is measured against the project management plan. Completion of the product scope is measured against the product requirements."* It also says that *"...the work of the project will result in delivery of the specified product scope."*[2] This is represented in Figure 8.2, so you can visually compare the product with the project scope.

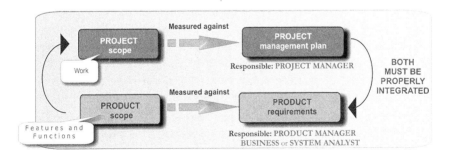

Figure 8.2 Measurement of project and product scope

---

2   *PMBOK® Guide*—Fifth Edition. 106.

I was talking with a project manager who manages complex projects in the banking industry for external customers. She asked me questions about the WBS, trying to clarify her understanding of it to improve her scope management. *"It's almost all about scope and how to better manage it. The scope is the basis for planning.* **Most arguments with the customer end up being around scope changes, scope expectations, requirements and such,"** she said. She mentioned issues often found in product and project scope management and the stress that certain kind of complex projects or industries create. We concluded that tools like the WBS help project managers to deal with that.

It's important to be careful when selling projects without a good scope definition and then expecting the project manager and team to meet unrealistic deadlines and to carry unreasonable workloads. There has to be a fair and realistic match between the sales process and the planning process; otherwise, the chances of failure are almost certain. You could execute a project without a good scope definition once or twice, or to gain a client in the short term, but you'll burn out yourself or your team if you don't work with a well-defined project and product scope.

Unfortunately this is not a rare instance. It may also explain why many projects still fail in spite of having more knowledge, tools, and skilled project managers. It's easy to blame the project manager for decisions outside his or her authority, or for decisions made even before assigning the project manager, but it isn't right. A survey from PriceWaterhouseCoopers says that *"top and senior management frequently blame project managers for bad project management and poor project results.* **There seems to be a belief amongst most organizations that no matter what happens, if the project fails, the project manager is always guilty**... *And yet, we can see from the survey that many of the reasons for project failure are organizationally related and are outside the direct range of influence of project managers."*[3] This is why it's important to talk more about the scope definition at the very early stages of a project, when sponsors, customers, and other stakeholders are setting deadlines and negotiating the product or service to deliver.

---

3   Evrard and Nieto. *Boosting business performance through program and project management.* 9 and 15.

WHAT'S THE ROLE OF THE WBS IN THE SCOPE BASELINE, AND SCOPE CHANGE CONTROL?

One of the key reasons why the WBS and WBS dictionary are so important is because both of them, together with the scope statement, are part of what is called the **scope baseline**, that I represent in Figure 8.3.

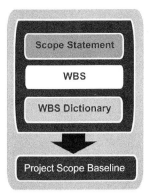

Figure 8.3 Project scope baseline

> **practical tip**
>
> *The scope baseline is part of the project management plan and once it's approved, it represents the approved project scope. It helps to determine if the requests for scope changes or additional work are inside or outside the project boundaries whenever those changes arise.*

The **scope statement** is another concept related to the scope baseline that includes the definition of the product scope, the project deliverables, and the definition of the product user acceptance criteria.

Consider that your current project is to build a house. You have the scope baseline and your customer requests to create a garage in the house. You refer to the scope baseline to see if the garage was inside scope or not, and the garage isn't in scope. It isn't listed in the scope statement or WBS. You tell the customer that the garage isn't in your project plan. The customer needs to go through the **formal change control process, meaning a change request must be submitted, and if that is approved, you'll update the scope baseline** to include the new customer request. Figure 8.4 demonstrates this process.

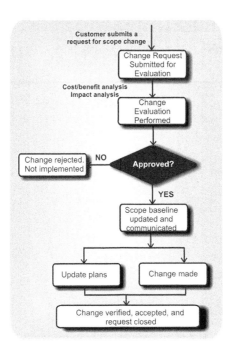

Figure 8.4 Scope change request submission

Now that you have an understanding of what each element of a scope baseline is, Figure 8.5 shows some of the processes (listed on the right side) that receive the scope baseline as an input, according to the *PMBOK® Guide*[4].

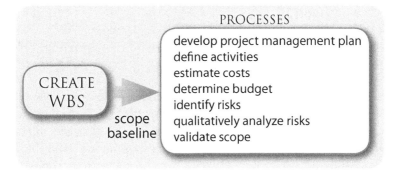

Figure 8.5 Processes that receive the scope baseline

This example shows that the scope baseline will directly influence the project management plan, activities definition, cost estimation, project budget, risk identification and risk qualitative analysis, and scope verification. **The influence of a well-defined WBS in the project planning is remarkable.** The better the WBS is, the better the project plan will be. The better your WBS is, the higher your chances are to have a good project plan, schedule, budget, risk register, and scope baseline.

In Figure 8.6 I graphically represent the *PMBOK® Guide[5]* processes belonging to the executing and monitoring and controlling groups that have change requests as an output.

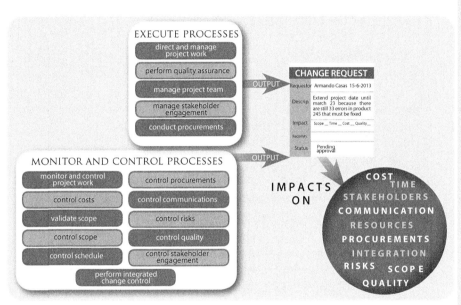

Figure 8.6 Processes with change requests as outputs

You might ask: *"what's the point?"* The point is that during the project execution or when you monitor and control the project, you may need to issue a change request. As a result of any of the processes shown in Figure 8.6, like controlling the scope or validating scope, one or more change requests may be needed. Change requests can have different impacts on the project. For example, some changes may impact the costs while others impact the quality or a combination of them. There could be a change request that impacts the project scope, and, as a result, impacts the WBS. Any of the 16 processes in Figure 8.6 could require updating the WBS and/or WBS dictionary. This figure represents what I described about the impact of change requests on the different project management areas. **During project execution, monitor**

5   *PMBOK® Guide*—Fifth Edition. 95.

ing or controlling, you need to update the WBS as a result of change requests. That should be done through the formal change control process, and the scope baseline will be updated.

HOW DO REQUIREMENTS AFFECT THE WBS?

Without well-defined project requirements, the chances to succeed with planning and execution decrease. The project scope can't be complete if you have poorly defined requirements. Let me introduce a few definitions before proceeding.

*"**Requirements** include the quantified and documented needs and expectations of the sponsor, customer, and other stakeholders."*[6]

The same way you have project scope and product scope, you have project requirements and product requirements.

* ❀ **Project requirements** have to do with business, delivery, and project management.
* ❀ **Product requirements** are related to technical aspects, security, safety, compliance, performance, quality, functions, and features.

The *PMBOK® Guide* includes a process called Collect Requirements, and the requirements documentation[7] is an input to create the WBS. Given this book focuses on the WBS not on requirements, I am not going to address requirements management, but the said input shows that it's critical to have requirements documentation while creating a valuable WBS.

"A high-quality WBS is constructed so that it can be used to meet all project requirements."[8] Given the tight relationship between requirements and scope, I'll mention a few things that are important to keep in mind. One tip is to involve business or systems analysts on your project team because they are masters at managing requirements. I've had great opportunities to work with senior business analysts who were responsible for managing the project requirements and it really made a difference. Even though scope management is a process where other stakeholders are involved, there should be a

---

6   *PMBOK® Guide*—Fifth Edition. 112. Author bolded certain words in original quote for the purpose of this book.

7   *PMBOK® Guide*—Fifth Edition. 125.

8   *Practice Standard for WBS*—Second Edition. 20.

very good interaction between the project manager and analysts.

Another thing to remember is that when you properly manage project requirements, it helps you better deal with customer expectations. You can influence the project's success by the level of effort you put into properly managing requirements. I've also found that **business analysts are key players when creating the WBS** because, as they are responsible for the requirements specification document, they bring great knowledge, expertise, and contributions into the work definition.

Related to requirements, there is a tool called the **Requirements Traceability Matrix,** which is a table to link project requirements with the requirement originator and allows requirements tracking. For example, you can know who requested each requirement, when, what priority was assigned to them, and other information. You can link the requirements with the WBS through this matrix. Table 8.1 shows an example of such a matrix which also traces the requirements to its corresponding WBS deliverables.

REQUIREMENTS TRACEABILITY MATRIX					
WBS ID	Req. ID	Requirement name	Owner	Priority	Comments
1.2.1	120	The system must support user administration to include multiple user and group roles.	Tom	High	
1.2.2	121	The system must support announcements on the home page.	Linda	High	To include maintenance
1.2.1	122	The system must support the creation, maintenance, and participation in surveys.	Luis	Medium	
1.2.1	123	The system must support the creation, maintenance, and participation in discussions.	Jon	Medium	
1.2.2.	145	The system must support the creation, maintenance, and participation in blogs.	Sharon	High	
1.2.1	146	The system must support the promotion of recently added books.	Patricia	Low	

Table 8.1 Requirements Traceability Matrix linked to the WBS

The Requirements Traceability Matrix helps you track the requirements throughout the project and manage changes to the product scope. It ensures that each requirement adds value to the business and that you'll deliver the approved requirements. Table 8.1 has a column titled Req. ID. This column applies a unique identification number to each requirement in the matrix. Each requirement also includes a name, its owner (the person who requested the requirement), its priority, and comments.

Take note of the column for t**he WBS ID which links each requirement with the WBS deliverables**. The WBS ID will ensure that all the requirements in the matrix have a corresponding approved deliverable in the WBS. Given many requirements can belong to the same deliverable, you'll find the same WBS ID in several rows corresponding to different requirements. So the Req. ID field contains unique numbers but the WBS ID doesn't have unique numbers in this matrix.

Via this matrix you can see all the requirements belonging to the same deliverable. For example, requirements numbered 120, 122, 123, and 156 belong to the same deliverable whose WBS ID is 1.2.1. You don't have the name of the 1.2.1 deliverable, but if you refer to the WBS, you'll see that the deliverable is the Website Release 1. That means that all the requirements 120, 122, 123, and 156 will be delivered in the first release of the website that the project is creating. There is another deliverable which is 1.2.2, Website Final Release, and it'll have requirements 121 and 145. Note that this isn't a complete matrix but a sample from a real-world project I managed in a Web development. However, this matrix can be used in other industries as well, if not in all of them.

WHAT IS OUT OF SCOPE?

It's as important to explicitly describe what's **IN scope** as it is to explicitly describe what's **OUT of scope.** The WBS documents components that are inside of the project scope but you also need to have a document describing those things that are excluded from the project scope. The **scope exclusions** aren't part of the WBS but you can add the list of exclusions in any project document, including in a representation of the WBS.

Figure 8.7 Out-of-scope representation

> *practical tip*
>
> *Explicitly stating what is outside of project scope helps you manage expectations regarding the project boundaries and avoids misunderstandings.*

The out-of-scope list (Figure 8.8) helps to clarify assumptions and understanding when documenting and communicating the scope with stakeholders and especially with customers. The list of things excluded from the scope can be distributed with the WBS so your stakeholders won't only receive what it's inside of scope, but also what it's outside of it. In my projects, when I use a tabular WBS representation in a spreadsheet, I often reserve a place at the end of it to describe the scope exclusions.

When you review the WBS with the stakeholders, you should also review the out-of-scope list, to make sure all the stakeholders agree with the things that are excluded from the scope.

NOT IN SCOPE LIST

Registration support
Sponsorship sales
Exhibitor sales
Website
Photography
Brochure designs

Figure 8.8 Out-of-scope list

HOW DOES THE WBS FIT IN WITH THE *PMBOK®GUIDE*?

It's important for you to understand how the WBS fits in with the *PMBOK® Guide,* as well as some of its related concepts. Please allow me to share a bit of theory at this point, as it's important to master the theory associated with the concepts you use.

Creating a WBS is in the Scope Management Knowledge Area within the *PMBOK® Guide*.

The **project scope management** *"includes the processes required to ensure that the project includes all the work required, and only the work required, to complete the project successfully. Managing the scope is primarily concerned with defining and controlling what is and is not included in the project."[9]*

I created Figure 8.9 to describe the scope management processes. The table shows how these processes fit within the *PMBOK® Guide's*[10] process groups (Initiation, Planning, Executing, Monitoring and Controlling, and Closing).

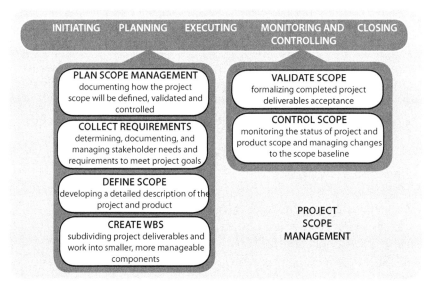

Figure 8.9 Fit of scope management processes in *PMBOK® Guide's* process groups

Remember, the WBS is referenced and used throughout the project. You can create it during the project initiation and/or planning, but you'll also use it when you execute, monitor, control, or close the project. Even though none of the scope processes are shown in the Initiating process group, the *PMBOK® Guide* says that *"within the Initiating processes, the initial scope is defined."[11]* It's during the project planning when you spend most of the effort to develop the WBS

9   *PMBOK® Guide*—Fifth Edition. 105.
10   *PMBOK® Guide*—Fifth Edition. 61.
11   *PMBOK® Guide*—Fifth Edition. 424.

and when you establish the **total project scope**; however, you can start working on the **initial scope** definition during the project initiation. I visually represent these concepts in Figure 8.10.

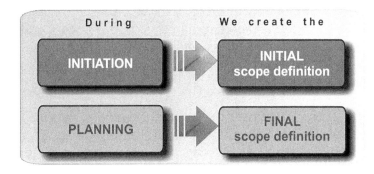

Figure 8.10 When to create the initial and final scope definitions

As shown in Figure 8.9, when you plan the project, you'll plan the scope management, collect the project requirements, define the project scope, and create the WBS. When you're monitoring and controlling the project, you'll validate and control the scope. This is how the WBS and scope fits into the *PMBOK® Guide's* project management process groups and Knowledge Areas.

practical tip

You don't need to wait until the beginning of the planning to start creating the WBS.

Figure 8.11 Scope management processes during planning

For you to create the WBS, you need to have the requirements documentation that comes from the Collect Requirements process. You need the scope statement that comes from the Define Scope process. Finally, you need other organizational process assets coming from the organization that executes the project.

You've concluded one of the fundamental chapters regarding how to effectively manage the project scope, the product scope, exclusions from scope, the importance of requirements within scope management and the creation of the WBS, and the relationship and influence of scope planning toward successful project management.

It's especially important for projects managers to know how to manage the scope baseline and process scope change requests. Based on the information and examples presented, you now have a good understanding to effectively manage your project scope and to create a useful WBS.

Similar to the way I discussed the integration between the WBS and scope management, I'll discuss in the next chapter, how to integrate the WBS with the schedule and costs, and how you can manage the schedule baseline.

chapter 9

How Do You Integrate the WBS with the Schedule and Costs?

One of the secrets about succeeding with the WBS is being able to effectively integrate the WBS with the project schedule and costs.

We've reached a point in the book and topic that I like because I clarify how to integrate, in practice, the WBS with the project schedule and cost. Here, the WBS makes a lot of sense to help maximize results and benefits. I also show how the WBS will help you to define the project activities once you start creating the schedule, and after you have your WBS complete. One of the key benefits you'll gain from this chapter is to learn how to use and apply the schedule baseline, and how it relates to scope management and the WBS. Managing the various project baselines is a must for high-performing project managers. In this chapter, I answer the following questions:

❀ What's the difference between the WBS and the schedule?

❀ Why should you link the WBS with the schedule?

❀ How can you link the WBS with the schedule?

❀ How can you link the WBS with costs?
> How you can use the WBS in cost estimating?
> How can you use the WBS to create the budget?

WHAT IS THE DIFFERENCE BETWEEN THE WBS AND THE SCHEDULE?

To respond this question, I'll first define a few concepts:

❀ **Schedule** is an organized list of activities and milestones. Each activity or milestone has specific information like duration, human or material resources assigned to it, start and end date. It is usually presented in a tabular form.

❀ **Task** is an activity to be accomplished within a defined period of time.

❀ **Gantt chart** is a graphical display of schedule-related information. It's a typical bar chart with dates shown across the top, activities and/or WBS components listed down the left side, and activity durations shown as date-placed horizontal bars.

I created Figure 9.1 and its subsequent comparison chart (Table 9.1) to represent and explain the major differences between a WBS and a schedule.

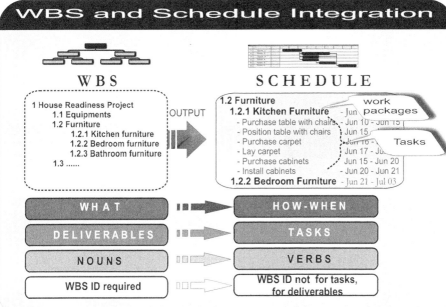

Figure 9.1 bg® key differences between the WBS and the schedule

Figure 9.1 lists key differences between the WBS and the schedule as detailed below:

❀ **WHAT versus HOW**. While the WBS represents the what of the project, meaning the work to be delivered to achieve the end goal, the schedule represents the how of the project, meaning how you are going to do the work and when— the means to the end goal. The WBS doesn't represent sequencing or dependencies among work.

PMI's *Practice Standard for WBS* reinforces this concept saying that the WBS *"is not a description of a process or schedule that defines how or when the deliverables will be produced, but rather is specifically limited to describing and detailing the project's outcome or scope.*"*

❀ **NOUNS versus VERBS.** While the WBS is written using nouns and adjectives to name its components, the schedule is written using verbs to name the activities or tasks.

---

* *Practice Standard for WBS*—Second Edition. 3.

❇ **DELIVERABLE orientation versus TASK orientation**. The WBS is oriented to deliverables, while the schedule is oriented to tasks. Thus, you'll not find tasks in a WBS, you'll find them only in the schedule. While the WBS can't have tasks, the schedule can have WBS components to show how you'll execute the work. See the third story in chapter 3.

Something else that you can see in Figure 9.1 is how the WBS helps to define the activities after it's created. The work package 1.2.1 Kitchen Furniture provides the framework to define the schedule activities corresponding to it like purchase and position table with chairs, or purchase and lay carpet. All the activities required to create the 1.2.1 deliverable inherit the deliverable WBS ID. All the activities corresponding to the 1.2.1 Kitchen Furniture deliverable will have a WBS ID 1.2.1 in the schedule which shows their WBS parent.

WBS AND SCHEDULE COMPARISON CHART

The three variations discussed are the major differences between the WBS and the schedule. However, there are a few more differences between them illustrated in Table 9.1

WBS AND SCHEDULE COMPARISON CHART		
	WBS	**SCHEDULE**
Graphical representation		
Work	Defines WHAT to deliver, what work is in scope	Defines HOW and WHEN the work will be executed
Purpose	Ultimate vision or goal. Products, services or results to deliver	Roadmap to achieve the deliverables
Orientation	Deliverables	Tasks, activities, actions
Component naming	Nouns and adjectives	Verbs
WBS ID	Yes	Optional. A well-defined WBS has it to link it with the schedule
Created by	Project Manager with stakeholders	Project Scheduler (sometimes is a role of the Project Manager)
Work sequencing	No	Yes
Creation order	The WBS is created first	The schedule is created after the WBS
Baseline	Scope baseline	Schedule baseline
Project area	Scope Management	Time Management
Process group	Initiation / Planning (to establish the scope)	Planning (to create the schedule)

Table 9.1 WBS and schedule comparison chart

PMI's *Practice Standard for Scheduling* says that *"The purpose of scheduling is to provide a 'roadmap' that represents how and when the project will deliver the products defined in the project scope."*[1] This definition reinforces what I presented above about the WBS being the **what** of the project and the schedule being the **how**. The illustration also shows how the WBS feeds into the schedule as the WBS is created first and during the Initiating process and the schedule is created during the Planning process.

Figure 9.2 represents the relationship between key components of scope management and time management. It shows how the WBS, the WBS dictionary, and the scope statement are related to the list of activities and the schedule. It also depicts **the WBS as an input to the schedule**. It helps define the activities. First, create the WBS. Then, define the activities. Use the WBS to determine which activities are needed to deliver each work package. **The activity list is an output** of this step. Once the list of activities is developed, you can sequence the activities as well as estimate resources and duration to generate the schedule. Even though the WBS is shown as an input to the processes of Define Activities and Develop Schedule, *"the activity list, WBS, and WBS dictionary **can be developed either sequentially or concurrently**, with the WBS and WBS dictionary being the basis for development of the final activity list."*[2]

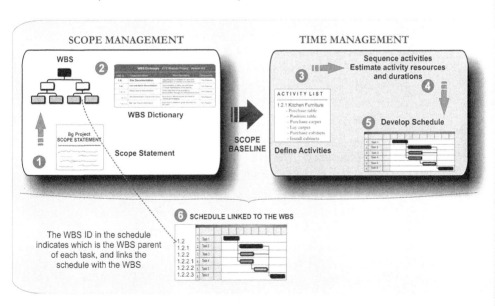

Figure 9.2 Scope and Time Management key components relationship

1   *Practice Standard for Scheduling*—Second Edition. 1.
2   *Practice Standard for WBS*—Second Edition. 17. Author bolded certain words in original quote for the purpose of this book.

WHY SHOULD YOU LINK THE WBS WITH THE SCHEDULE?

PMI's *Practice Standard for Scheduling* describes why you should link the WBS with the schedule in this way: "...**to ensure that all aspects of the project scope have been adequately defined and included in the schedule** model. *Activities in the schedule model represent the work that produces the work packages identified in the WBS; thus,* **all work elements in the WBS should be directly traceable to a schedule activity or group of activities**. *Conversely, each activity should roll up into only one WBS element.*"[3]

Note that there is a way to trace the WBS with the activities. You do that through the WBS ID. Insert a column into the schedule to add the WBS ID corresponding to each group of activities. I'll share two key reasons why l**inking the WBS with the schedule leads to better project results**. Let my real-life examples serve as proof as to why linking the WBS with the schedule brings better awareness earlier in the project for things you wouldn't have realized otherwise.

The two benefits I observed of linking the WBS with the schedule are:

1. Allows you to **make sure that all the work defined in the WBS has an associated plan (schedule) and will be executed**. Thus, you won't miss pieces of work during execution. All the work that was approved will have a plan and will be executed. How you can ensure that? Because you'll check that all the deliverables in the WBS have their associated activities in the schedule and will be executed.
2. Allows you to **make sure that only the approved work will be executed**. No work outside of scope will be executed. How? If you have in the schedule something that isn't in the WBS or can't be linked to any deliverable in the WBS, then it must not be in the schedule.

In a project I managed, I was responsible for the project **master schedule**, which was the schedule covering all the main aspects of the project and major integrations. Given the project had an important number of technical deliverables, I managed the master schedule while a technical leader was responsible for the **technical**

---

3   *Practice Standard for Scheduling*—Second Edition. 15. Author bolded certain words in original quote for the purpose of this book.

schedule which detailed the technical milestones that I had in my master schedule. The master schedule had 350 tasks and the technical schedule had 550 tasks. The project duration was less than a year. When I assigned the work to the technical leader, I shared the WBS and we discussed it. The leader and his team created the technical schedule. When the technical schedule was complete, the leader sent it to me for feedback, and the first thing I did was to make sure that:

1. Everything that was in the WBS had corresponding tasks in the technical schedule, and
2. Only approved work from the WBS had been included in the technical schedule.

To ensure that all work associated with WBS deliverables would be executed, I reviewed each work package against both the master and technical schedules to ensure they had associated tasks in the schedules. After the revision, I realized that not all the work packages had an associated group of tasks in one of the schedules. That meant I was missing some pieces of work that wouldn't be executed and delivered. For example, we were purchasing a Web conferencing solution which had to be integrated with an audio solution. Both solutions were in the WBS. However, the work related to the audio solution was missing in the technical schedule. What would be the impact in the project or to the customer if we hadn't realized that when we did? We would have delivered a Web conferencing solution without audio capabilities!

When I realized that the audio integration piece was missing, I asked the leader to add it to the technical schedule. This is the kind of situation where is useful to check if all the work in the WBS was actually planned. Sometimes, the project manager is responsible for the entire project schedule, but other times, the project scheduler or other leaders are responsible for creating specific schedules related to a master schedule. The leaders and the project manager are responsible to make sure all the schedules integrate well with each other. **It's important that the master schedule is aligned not only with the WBS, but also with other related schedules (like sub-project schedules).** This situation of having more than one schedule applies more to bigger and complex projects, or those with several sub-teams.

To ensure that only the approved work will be executed, we reviewed all the schedules tasks and confirmed their corresponding work package. The WBS ID which was shared among the WBS components and corresponding activities made it easy to cross reference this. While doing so, I realized that some groups of tasks in the schedule had no corresponding work package in the WBS. I couldn't assign a WBS ID to those tasks to link the schedule with the WBS. That meant that **I found in the technical schedule planned tasks that weren't in the approved scope**. Those tasks didn't have an associated work package in the WBS. Figure 9.3 shows an example of this. Pay attention to the first column labeled WBS ID where it says "OUT OF SCOPE" or "OUTSIDE SCOPE".

WBS Id	❶	Task Name	Trabajo	Duración
1.3.8		⊟ Corporate Site Changes	82 hrs	21 días
1.3.8.1		⊟ Modification and Implementation of My	82 hrs	21 días
	🔳	Enable Part to Support Links [Already in	42 hrs	6 días
	🔳	Feed from Orgs as well as Component S	40 hrs	5.71 días
		⊞ User Administration	92 hrs	13.04 días
		⊞ Dynamic feature deployment	164 hrs	110.43 días
		⊟ Site Release 5	469.8 hrs	100.84 día
		⊟ Workflow System	0 hrs	100.84 días
OUT OF SCOPE		⊟ Versioning of Customized / Instantiated Workflo	0 hrs	2.86 días
OUT OF SCOPE		Develop and Unit Test Component (Save As - over	0 hrs	2.86 días
1.3.9		⊟ Custom Monitoring	0 hrs	12.14 días
1.3.9	🔳 ⟨	Document brief detailed speciifcation of solution	0 hrs	1.14 días
1.3.9		Force Timeouts - develop multiple test scenarios	0 hrs	0.29 días
1.3.9		Define the specific error numbers / messages to t	0 hrs	1.71 días
1.3.9		Define physical methods of trapping these errrors	0 hrs	1.14 días
1.3.9		Set up site scope alerts to proactively test for con	0 hrs	7.71 días
1.3.9		⊟ Alert / Notification Engine	0 hrs	4 días
1.3.9		Design document - basic queuing and deliver	0 hrs	1.71 días
1.3.9		Look up of Admin contact information by site	0 hrs	1.14 días
1.3.9		Notify site admin as well as central location	0 hrs	1.14 días
1.3.9		Test timeouts / Alert Functionality	0 hrs	1.14 días
OUTSIDE SCOPE		Usage Reporting / Statistics	0 hrs	5.71 días
OUTSIDE SCOPE		⊟ Chat	0 hrs	56.27 días
OUTSIDE SCOPE		⊟ User Directory / Profile	0 hrs	56.27 días
OUTSIDE SCOPE	🔳	Define Scope and Reqs	0 hrs	5.71 días
OUTSIDE SCOPE		D&U design [Incremental]	0 hrs	5.71 días
OUTSIDE SCOPE		Development Planning - Directory & Chat	0 hrs	1.71 días
OUTSIDE SCOPE		⊞ Chat Solution	0 hrs	43.14 días

Figure 9.3 Scheduled tasks which are out of the approved scope

As a result of my cross referencing, the team and I had to remove from the schedule the tasks that were out of scope, or determine why they were included in the schedule if they weren't approved. After I linked the schedule with the WBS, I talked with the technical leader to determine why those tasks outside of scope had been planned. *"If we don't do these tasks now, we'll have to do them next year anyway,"* he said. He explained that it was cost-effective to have the tasks in the scope at that time and his explanation made sense. After further evaluation, discussions, and negotiations, we got approval from the customer. Through formal scope change control, we added some of those tasks to the approved scope. We had to edit the WBS and related documents, and those tasks were added to the schedules. As for the tasks that weren't approved to become part of the scope, we removed them from the technical schedule. Linking the WBS with the schedule and vice-versa will enable you to have those discussions around scope to obtain better results.

> **practical tip**

Linking the WBS with the schedule is a very powerful way of managing the project scope and ensuring that all the scope is planned, and only the scope is planned.

HOW CAN YOU LINK THE WBS WITH THE SCHEDULE?

Now that you know the benefits of linking the schedule with the WBS, I'll share **how** you can link them in practice. The first thing you have to do in the schedule to link it with the WBS is to add a new field (column) for the WBS ID. The WBS ID field will contain the WBS ID of the WBS work package associated to the task in the schedule.

> **practical tip**

The way to link the WBS with the schedule is through the WBS ID.

For example, the work package 3.2.1.1 Flyer Translation Documents shown in Figure 9.4, delivers a series of documents with the Spanish version of a corporate flyer. This is a tangible and measurable deliverable, a series of documents with the text on the flyer in Spanish. The schedule will include all the tasks needed to deliver the Flyer Translation Documents. Those tasks are not in the WBS because the WBS has no tasks, but they are in the schedule as shown in Figure 9.4.

WBS Id	❶	Nombre de tarea	Duración	Comienzo	Fin
3.2.1.1		⊟ Flyer Translation Documents	18 días	8/17/2009	9/9/2009
3.2.1.1	✓	Create Translation Validation Team	3 días	8/17/2009	8/19/2009
3.2.1.1	✓	Define the Team Norms and Procedure for Translations	1 día	8/17/2009	8/17/2009
3.2.1.1		Send Translation to the Team for validation	0 días	8/19/2009	8/19/2009
3.2.1.1		Receive input from Team	5 días	8/20/2009	8/26/2009
3.2.1.1		Process input from Team	10 días	8/27/2009	9/9/2009
3.2.1.1		Send final approved version of translation	0 días	9/9/2009	9/9/2009

Figure 9.4 WBS ID in a project schedule

Figure 9.4 first column shows that the same WBS ID can be associated to more than one task in the schedule because one deliverable could need many tasks to be implemented. As a result, **all the tasks needed to implement a deliverable are linked to the same WBS ID, which is the deliverable WBS ID**. The deliverable WBS ID is the parent for those tasks. In the example, all the tasks corresponding to the 3.2.1.1 deliverable will have the same WBS ID in the schedule.

It's simple to link the WBS and the schedule, and doing so can benefit projects. In bigger projects, it's sometimes harder to check if you have planned for all the approved work. It could be time-consuming depending on the quantity of tasks included in the schedule— even though this is done only once. It's generally completed once the WBS is approved, unless the scope changes significantly. The benefits of linking the WBS with the schedule exceed the effort.

Something else to note in Figure 9.4 is that all the tasks are named with verbs: create, define, send, receive, and process. However, the work package or deliverable doesn't contain a verb in its name, just nouns and adjectives. I've made this point several times throughout this book and now have drawn your attention to a real-world example of that.

> *good practice*
>
> *Map each schedule activity with the WBS via the WBS ID, and make sure all the WBS deliverables have corresponding activities in the schedule.*

Finally, I offer evidence to the practice of linking the WBS with the schedule through the WBS ID. PMI's *Practice Standard of Scheduling* defines this as a good practice saying that the WBS ID *"maps the activity or task to the project WBS. Defines the 'parent element' of the task within the WBS."*[4]

---

4   *Practice Standard for Scheduling—Second Edition.* 45.

HOW CAN YOU LINK THE WBS WITH COSTS?

The WBS is related to some aspects of project cost management, especially in the areas of cost estimating and budgeting. Let's explore these relationships. The scope baseline is an input to cost estimating and cost budgeting processes. As a result, given that the WBS and the WBS dictionary are part of the scope baseline, the WBS and the WBS dictionary are also inputs to estimate the project costs and to create the budget. Figure 9.5 shows the scope baseline as an input to the processes to obtain the project budget.

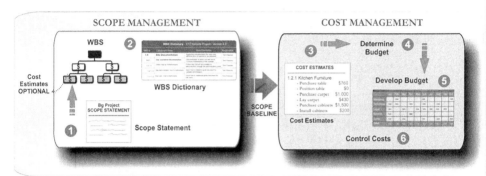

Figure 9.5 WBS and WBS Dictionary as inputs for Cost Management

Figure 9.5 doesn't intend to show all the inputs and outputs of the processes of estimating costs and determining budget. It just presents the role of the scope baseline in cost management. It also shows that the cost estimates could be developed during the project planning or you could optionally receive the cost estimates as an input from the WBS if the cost estimates were entered in the WBS. Oftentimes, it's a mix, meaning the WBS has its initial cost estimates assigned to the work packages (and rolled up to the higher levels), and during project planning the WBS is used as an input, in addition estimates are refined as new information is available. After that, the budget is created.

HOW YOU CAN USE THE WBS IN COST ESTIMATING?

When you **estimate costs**, you approximate the costs that you need to achieve the different project elements.

One of the uses of the WBS is to produce the cost estimates for the project by assigning an individual cost estimate to each work package. This is great because the WBS presents the total scope of work. That means you'll have the cost estimates for the entire project! Your chances of running into cost overruns decrease because you're capturing all the work and are estimating what the cost is to complete the entire scope and all the deliverables. **A well-defined WBS is an incredible help in estimating the project cost and effort**. You'll make sure through the WBS that you have estimated the cost for the total scope of work.

> *practical tip*

To show the cost estimates in the WBS, insert an additional field called cost or cost estimate.

Figure 9.6 is a representation of the translations project described in chapter 5. The assumption is that to do the Flyers Translations in Spanish, one person and eight hours are needed. The hourly rate is $60. With this information you know that to achieve the Spanish Flyers Translations, you need a budget of $480. Based on that, you'll update the WBS to enter the cost estimate for component 1.2.1.1. In the same way, you can enter the cost estimates for all the components in the WBS.

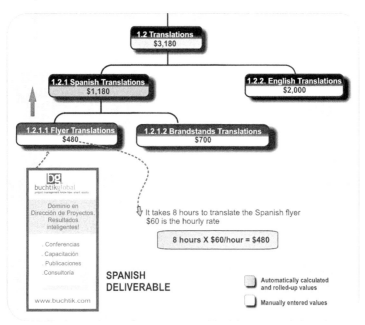

Figure 9.6 WBS with cost estimates

After the estimated cost for the Spanish flyer and brandstands translations are entered, the estimates are rolled up and the cost for the Spanish Translations totals $1,180—which is the sum of $480 and $700. Once you know the cost estimates for the English and Spanish Translations, you'll know the total cost for translations as a whole, which is the sum of $1,180 and $2,000. Thus, $3,180 is the total estimated cost for the project to deliver the translations deliverables.

You'll stop decomposing the work in the WBS at the work package level, which is where you can estimate the project cost and time. You can use the work packages to estimate the different costs needed, including those for human resources, materials, and project management efforts like the implementation of a risk response strategy. Figure 9.6 also shows that cost estimates are entered into each individual work package. Many software tools for WBSs roll up the costs to higher levels to produce the total project cost estimate.

The WBS dictionary is useful in cost management because it provides valuable information that can help better develop estimates that are more realistic and accurate. For example, the WBS could indicate the materials of a deliverable or items that need to be estimated.

HOW CAN YOU USE THE WBS TO CREATE THE PROJECT BUDGET?

Using the WBS in determining the budget ensures that you'll plan for the necessary funds to complete the work for each deliverable. One of the techniques used to determine the budget is cost aggregation. **Cost aggregation** consists of aggregating the cost estimates per work package according to the WBS. Since cost estimates have already been made at the work package level and rolled up to the higher levels of the WBS, it's only a matter of consolidating the costs into the budget. If you use software to define the WBS, you can easily start creating your budget based on the cost estimates entered in the WBS. To do that, you have to export the WBS into a spreadsheet. Several WBS software tools allow exporting to spreadsheets.

This concludes one of the richest chapters in this book. Now, the challenge is to start linking your WBS with your schedule and budget, if you haven't done so already. I encourage you to start taking advantage of the benefits and results associated with this good practice.

In the next chapter you will learn how to link the WBS with other project areas.

chapter 10

How Do You Use the WBS with Communications, Risks, Acquisitions, Human Resources, Stakeholders and Quality?

The WBS is not just a matter of helping us to better manage the scope. There are many more uses of it outside of scope management that improve project results.

The WBS not only helps you manage the scope, as discussed throughout this book, but also assists you with managing several other project areas. This chapter shows the relationship between the WBS and these other areas—communications, risks, procurement, human resources, quality, and stakeholders— and you'll see how to quickly take advantage of these integrations for the benefit of your project. The questions I'lldiscuss in the context of a project include:

❋ How do you use the WBS in Communications?
❋ How do you use the WBS in Risks?
❋ How do you use the WBS in Acquisitions?
❋ How do you use the WBS in Human Resources?
❋ How do you use the WBS in Quality?
❋ How do you use the WBS with Stakeholders?

HOW DO YOU USE THE WBS IN COMMUNICATIONS?

In this section I address how to improve project scope-related communications by using different color-coding in the WBS. I also treat how to better plan the project communications considering the scope, and provide an example of a communications plan.

The WBS is very valuable not only to communicate the scope of work or its changes, but also to serve as a **powerful reporting tool** and to include other project information, like project progress and status. One of the best ways to leverage the WBS for your communications and reporting is to use colors within it. This section addresses the following questions:

- ❀ How do you improve communications by using color-coding in the WBS?
  - > How do you use colors at each WBS level?
  - > How do you use colors at each release?
  - > How do you use colors to identify progress?
  - > How do you use colors to indicate acquisitions?
- ❀ What are the other uses of the WBS in communications?
- ❀ How do you use the WBS with the communications plan?

HOW DO YOU IMPROVE COMMUNICATIONS BY USING COLOR CODING IN THE WBS?

What I discovered through the use of colors and icons in the WBS has made a difference in my projects' communications. The use of different colors in the WBS components helps in many ways, especially when presenting or reporting scope related information. What follows is a series of examples of how I use them, and discover new ways to use the WBS.

HOW DO YOU USE COLORS AT EACH WBS LEVEL?

The simplest way to use colors at each WBS level is to assign a different color for each level. For instance, Figure 10.1 shows how Level 1, Level 2, Level 3, and Level 4 are all in different colors.

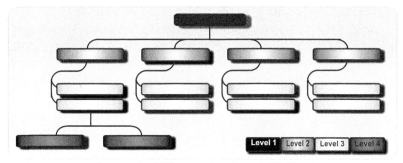

Figure 10.1 Different colors in each WBS level

This makes it fast and easy for stakeholders and the project team to recognize each WBS level at a glance. It helps clarify the different levels when dealing with big projects and large WBSs.

Depending on the software used to create the WBS, you may decide to have a high-level WBS in one page or file, and then decompose each of the branches in different pages or files. In this case, each page or file contains the decomposition of each individual branch or a set of branches. When you connect the pages and review the different files, the colored levels help to quickly visualize each level.

HOW DO YOU USE COLORS AT EACH RELEASE?

In some industries, especially in iterative development projects, the scope of the work often is increased related to the different product releases to the customer. In this context, it's good to use color in the WBS to identify the distinct pieces of work that will be delivered with each release. For example, work shown with a blue background is associated with the first release, work indicated with a green background is associated with the second release, and a yellow background indicates work associated with the final release.

HOW DO YOU USE COLORS TO IDENTIFY PROGRESS?

You can use different colors to highlight the progress of work and deliverables in the WBS. Figure 10.2 shows a section of a tabular WBS of a business project with color coding to denote progress.

For example, components in blue can identify the deliverables that are complete. Those in green identify the components in progress. White components show the work that has not been addressed yet.

8 Locations and Travel	8.1 Congress Registry			Tom
	8.2 Trip package			Tom
	8.3 Speaker's agenda			Patricia
	8.4 Hotel reservations			Susana
	8.5 Flight reservations			Susana
	8.6 Transfer reservations			Susana
	8.7 Visas			Susana
	8.8 Tours reservations			Susana
9 Congress Dashboard	9.1 Success Metrics	9.1.1	Dashboard template	Abigail
		9.1.2	Success metrics template	Patricia
		9.1.3	Metrics comparison	Patricia
	9.2 Satisfaction Survey	9.2.1	eSurvey template	Patricia
		9.2.2	eSurvey logistics	Abigail
		9.2.3	eSurvely implementation	Luis
		9.2.4	eSurvey results	Luis

On Time   Not started   Completed   At Risk

Figure 10.2 Different colors per component to indicate progress

With this, the WBS becomes a tool to help better manage the project performance. It provides a picture of the deliverables and completed components versus those that are still in progress. Of course, the schedule reflects progress. However, executives and sponsors, for example, generally don't review long and detailed schedules. They prefer to see a snapshot of progress for major deliverables. The WBS becomes a tool to compare the scope that was planned versus the scope that has been accomplished.

HOW DO YOU USE COLORS TO INDICATE ACQUISITIONS?

The strategies for managing providers and internal project teams often differ. Whatever strategy you use, be sure to **clearly identify work that will be executed in-house and work that will be executed through outside vendors. Basically, determine what will be acquired.** It's especially good to highlight outsourced work because contracts sometimes present risks like terms of the contract or providers missing deadlines. When the contracted items are highlighted or color coded on the WBS, the project manager, or the person responsible to manage contracts, easily can see and track those components. I usually identify procured elements with a different color not only for my benefit, but also so I can **clearly show my team and stakeholders the procured deliverables so they will understand why those components are not further decomposed on our WBS** since the provider will decompose them.

Figure 10.3 shows a simplified version of a WBS where we had acquisitions with different vendors to provide prototypes of a solution. We managed a procurement process to select a vendor to provide a Web conferencing solution and we implemented the integration of the solution with our corporate website. We contracted an expert provider to analyze a series of requirements. Finally, we procured the design and usability of the website we were releasing. All those **components to be acquired externally are highlighted with a different color in the WBS and noted in the legend as "buy" components.**

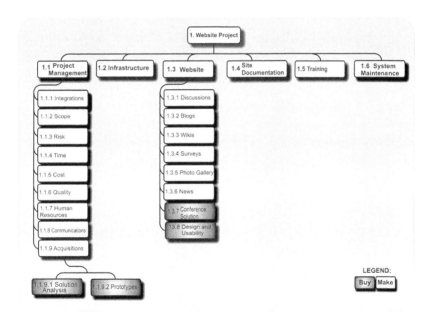

Figure 10.3 Use of colors to identify WBS procured components– Option A

Color coding external components also helps to visualize where you'll have **work integration, assembly points, or interfaces** with external subprojects. It's important to mention these interfaces because to successfully manage the interfaces with other subprojects you need to define associated work in the WBS. For example, if you buy a Web conferencing system, you'll need to have work defined in the WBS related to the integration testing of the acquired system with the internal systems.

WHAT ARE THE OTHER USES OF THE WBS TO ASSIST WITH COMMUNICATIONS?

One aspect to consider while creating the WBS is to identify and include any deliverables about special reports or communications. For example, in a procurement process I managed, we didn't have in scope to create an executive report about the procurement process we were following. However, the sponsors requested this report to show the customers how we managed the procurement from beginning to end. Due to its importance, we had to involve various individuals from the project team for a few days to work on the creation, validation, and approval of the report before it went out to the customers. As this communication wasn't initially in scope, it impacted the use of the resources and in projects with tight deadlines this could be an issue. You may want to **identify key communications as deliverables in your WBS**.

In other chapters of the book, I discussed several ideas about the WBS that I would like to review again now in the context of communication. These concepts include:

- The WBS helps you manage expectations and avoid misunderstandings and misconceptions about the project scope and result (chapter 5).
- Some software tools make creating and modifying the WBS easy. Software can also help you add visual elements to simplify the communication efforts, as well as to present the scope in details or at a summary level depending on your stakeholder's reporting needs (chapter 7).
- Finally, the WBS not only helps you identify what is in and out of scope, but also communicate that to stakeholders (chapter 8).

To this final point, I offer the following advice. While the WBS is effective in identifying and communicating scope boundaries, it's important for you to **be sensitive when communicating scope**

boundaries. It's also relevant to recognize what power degree each stakeholder has and how you'll communicate the boundaries and when to consider their requests. Theory may say that if something is outside of scope, you should just inform the stakeholder that the request won't be performed. In practice though, if the highest executive of your organization or your customer requests something additional or new to the project, it's something that has to be considered. Someone once told me: *"if any stakeholder asks me for something that is not in scope, I just them that we will not do it."* That response wouldn't be wise when handling a request from a high executive or client. The stakeholder's request must be considered and a change request form should also be submitted so that the request's impact can be analyzed in order for the executive to make an informed decision.

While there are some stakeholders whose level of influence in the project is minor, there are others whose requests should be seriously considered. For example, during a construction project, an external stakeholder from an environmental organization requests to add something in the scope involving quality assurance of the project's environmental impact. It would not be prudent to respond by telling the environmental agent that the request is out of scope. The implications to your project would be far worse than making a change request. Your entire project could get shut down or not get approved. Our challenge as project managers is not only to manage the scope changes efficiently, but also to **communicate the scope boundaries and changes effectively.**

HOW DO YOU USE THE WBS WITH THE COMMUNICATIONS PLAN?

The communications management plan, also known as **communications plan**, determines the project information that the stakeholders need; it defines the project communication approach and indicates the information to be communicated. It includes format, content, level of detail, objective, audience, dates and/or frequency for distribution, person responsible for communicating, methods or technology used, language, pre-conditions, status (if that was communicated already or is pending), among other information. Table 10.1 shows a section of one communication plan for a project that I managed.

PARTIAL - **PROJECT COMMUNICATION PLAN**					
What to communicate	**Audience**	**Purpose**	**When Frequency**	**Mean or method**	**Responsible**
Initiation information	Customer, Sponsors, Team	Inform of scope, risks, plans, assumptions	Once. Kick-off	Kick-off meeting	Project Manager
Top Management Status Report	Program Mgr, Sponsors, Funcional Mgrs	Inform of status, risks, escalations, activities, key & upcoming	Every other Friday	Document sent by e-mail	Project Manager
Satus and Coordination Meeting	Sub-teams	Progress evaluation, status, coordination, issues	Daily	Face to face. 11-11:15am	Sub-team leaders
Sub-teams progress report	Project Manager	Progress versus plan. Scope Control	Every Monday	E-mail	Sub-team leaders
Change Control Review Meeting	Managers affected by the project	Review Change Control Forms	As Change Requests arise	Face to face meetings	Business Analyst, Project Manager

Table 10.1 Project Communications Plan

In the communications plan, it's important to identify the **stakeholders with whom you need to communicate the WBS, the WBS dictionary, or the scope baseline**. Table 10.1 indicates what will you communicate, to whom you will do it, what the purpose of the communication is, when will you communicate it, by which means, medium or technology you will do it, who the responsible is for the communication, and in which language he or she will communicate it. In situations where you wish to tell the stakeholders or the team about project scope, progress, status, accomplishments, and risks, the WBS is invaluable. One of the major reasons for project failures is communication barriers or issues about the project scope. Those issues can be minimized by using the WBS to properly communicate the scope and other performance information.

HOW DO YOU USE THE WBS IN RISKS?

The WBS is a valuable resource to assist in project risk management. This section presents how to use the WBS is risk management and how to highlight the major areas of risk within the scope. It shows how risks impact the WBS and how to link the risk register with the WBS **to track riskiest deliverables**. This section answers the following questions:

- How does the WBS helps with risk management?
- How do you display major risks in a WBS?
- What are the impacts of risk on the WBS?
- How do you link the risk registry with the WBS?

HOW DOES THE WBS HELPS IN RISK MANAGEMENT?

The WBS is one of the main sources and inputs to identify project risks. By analyzing the scope in the WBS, you can think what things could go wrong with each deliverable, which threats could prevent you from delivering a work package, and where you may find risks. For example, the project team could ask themselves:

- Do we have deployment risks associated with any of the WBS deliverables? or
- Do we have WBS deliverables to be developed in-house whose work is not part of our core business, and thus it might be less risky to outsource them?

You can be more effective in risk identification at the work package level to detect early warnings or threats by using the WBS while managing risks. You'll never be able to identify all the risks up front as there will always be unknown risks, those that you can't anticipate. However, the WBS will increase the chances of success in your risk management, and you'll be able to better predict as many risks as possible. While identifying risks you can **use the WBS as a checklist to make sure that you have reviewed all the project work to consider its potential risks**.

> *practical tip*
>
> *Use the WBS as a way to discuss potential risks associated with each deliverable.*

The WBS *"supports tracking of risks to assist the project manager in identifying and implementing responses necessary to achieve desired outcomes."*[1] The WBS helps in implementing risks responses like mitigation, avoidance, acceptance, and transference for negative risks, as well as responses for positive risks or opportunities.

---

1   Practice Standard for WBS—Second Edition. 7.

HOW DO YOU DISPLAY MAJOR RISKS IN A WBS?

You can use different colors to identify, highlight, and communicate only those WBS components that are riskiest. This way you will be able to focus on them first. Figure 10.4 shows an example. The example represents the major deliverables with risks which are those associated with the publisher contract and book printing— represented with dark boxes. Note that the WBS in this figure is not a Risk Breakdown Structure (RBS), as discussed in chapter 3. This is a WBS highlighting components with highest risks. The WBS can be used in conjunction with the RBS in risk management.

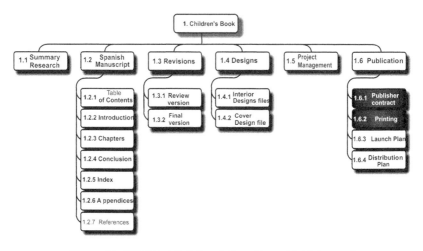

Figure 10.4 WBS highlighting deliverables with highest risks

HOW DO RISKS IMPACT THE WBS?

Project work and the WBS could need modifications as a result of risk responses. There may be risk response strategy that requires issuing a scope change request. For example, you have a WBS component to be created in-house with the company's resources but there is a risk of not meeting the deadline, given your staff is not experienced in the equipment needed to create the component. To mitigate that, you decide to outsource the component, which will lead to a change in the scope. This is an example of the considerations you need to make when managing risks and evaluating response strategies. **Before choosing a risk response, you should determine what the impact will be to the scope and to the WBS.**

HOW DO YOU LINK THE RISK REGISTER WITH THE WBS?

The **risk register** is a matrix used to manage project risks. Table 10.2 presents an example of it. The WBS could be linked to the risk register to determine which work packages have more risks associated.

BG PROJECT RISK REGISTER 10 MAY 2013								
Risk	**Cat.**	**Prob.**	**Impact**	**Score**	**Response strategy**	**Respon-sible**	**Due date**	**Status**
Due to lack of technical resources, there's a risk in the product development which could impact the schedule	Resources	Medium	High	High	Hire new resources. Release resources from lower-priority projects	Project Manager	5 May	Pending
Due to lack of experience in design and usability, users may find the product complex and thus reject it	Design	Low	High	Medium	Contract design and usability experts. Involve more customers in testing	Marketing Leader	30 June	Closed
Due to complex requirements, the development could be delayed, which would impact the delivery date or quality	Technical	High	Medium	High	Integrate with third party solution	Technical Leader	15 July	Pending
Due to the global and diverse audience, the product may not be applicable to all regions and thus not used consistently	Technical	Medium	High	High	Plan testing to cover countries where we have many customers	Quality Leader	7 Sept.	Pending

Table 10.2 Risk register example

The risk register lists information about the project risks like risk probability, impact, score (probability * impact), response strategies, risk owner, a due date and status of the risk, among others. The register is one of the key tools to manage risks. The team will first address the risks with higher score. The reason why I explained the risk register is because you can insert a WBS ID column in it to link the risk associated with each WBS deliverable. This helps **to identify if there are deliverables that have several risks associated with them,** and whether you may need to change the scope or look for options on delivering the work differently. For example, Table 10.2 shows the risks associated with the in-house implementation of a product. As a result, you may decide to remove the in-house development from scope and to procure it from a third party.

HOW DO YOU USE THE WBS IN ACQUISITIONS?

The WBS helps to effectively communicate the scope to providers, and to manage the project acquisition process. In this section I use the word procurement or acquisition to mean the same thing. The questions I discuss include:

- How can you use the WBS in procurement?
- How does the WBS help you with make-or-buy decisions?
- How do you use the WBS in buy-decisions?
- What's the relationship between the project WBS and the contract WBS?

HOW CAN YOU USE THE WBS IN PROCUREMENT?

*"**Project Procurement Management** includes the processes necessary to purchase or acquire products, services, or results needed from outside the project team… [It] includes the contract management and change control processes to develop and administer contracts or purchase orders."[2]*

The first process within procurement management is **plan procurement management** which is *"the process of documenting project purchasing decisions, specifying the approach, and identifying potential sellers."[3]* The first input to plan procurement management is the project management plan, and since the WBS is part of it, the WBS is a key input to this process. Every time you need to plan acquisitions, you must consider the WBS and its WBS dictionary, as they provide valuable information regarding deliverables to be acquired outside the organization. **The WBS is fundamental to create statements of work and contracts.**

The procurement management plan guides providers on how to develop and maintain a WBS. An example is the *MIL-STD-881A handbook* used by the U.S. Department of Defense. This handbook guides contractors and project managers to prepare, understand, extend and present a WBS, to ensure its consistent application.

---

2   *PMBOK® Guide*—Fifth Edition. 355. Author bolded certain words in original quote for the purpose of this book.
3   *PMBOK® Guide*—Fifth Edition. 355.

Further, the **WBS should be updated as a result of change requests that were approved based on the procurement plan**. For example, you determined to complete a work package in-house and that was reflected in the WBS. After procurement planning, you decided to buy that component instead of making it, thus, you'll need to change the scope and update the WBS to reflect the new decision.

HOW DOES THE WBS HELP YOU WITH MAKE-OR-BUY DECISIONS?

When you plan acquisitions, one of the important decisions is if you'll make a specific deliverable in-house, or if you'll buy it. This is known as a **make-or-buy decision**. When analyzing the project work, use the WBS to determine if it's best to make in-house or to acquire certain deliverables or subprojects externally.

Earlier in this chapter, Figure 10.3 presented a WBS with one option to represent the WBS components that would be acquired externally. I labeled that figure as Option A, which showed two procured components inside the WBS component 1.1.9 Acquisitions and two deliverables listed under 1.3 Website. Those four deliverables were indicated using a different color to identify deliverables acquired externally. The procured work appears there because components 1.3.7 Conference Solution as well as 1.3.8 Design and Usability are part of the website (represented as 1.3 Website). The components 1.1.9.1 Solution Analysis and 1.1.9.2 Prototypes are not part of the website itself. They are separate deliverables that will be acquired. As a result, those components appear under 1.1.9 Acquisitions because the project manager was responsible to manage that acquisition until successful delivery, but he was not responsible to manage the work inside those acquired packages.

SECRETS TO MASTERING THE WBS

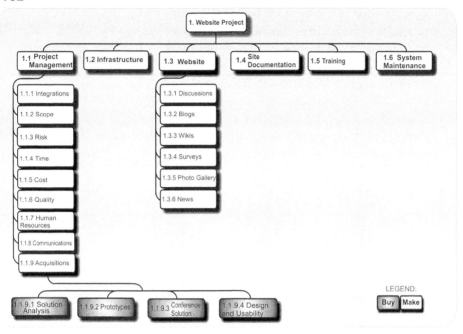

Figure 10.5 Colors to identify procured components – Option B

Using the same example, Figure 10.5 shows Option B, which is an alternate way of organizing the same work to be procured. This figure contains all the acquired components under 1.1.9 Acquisitions. If you are responsible for the acquisitions—indicated by the 1.1.9 Acquisitions component—and will manage these procurements, then all the procurement deliverables could be grouped inside 1.1.9. In my projects, I generally use Option B instead of Option A.

Providers receive only a high-level WBS of the components that they will provide. This is just to guide them on the product, service, or result that they will deliver. Dr. Kerzner suggests to *"develop a preliminary WBS to not lower than the top three levels for solicitation purposes… the contractor is required to extend the preliminary WBS in response to the solicitation…"*[4] This is also recommended by the U.S. Department of Defense: *"the top three levels are the minimum recommended any program or contract needs for reporting purposes unless the items identified are high cost or high risk."*[5]

---

4   Kerzner, H. *Project Management: A Systems Approach to Planning, Scheduling, and Controlling* – Tenth Edition. 442. *

5   [U.S.] *Department of Defense Handbook. Work Breakdown Structures for Defense Materiel Items*, MIL-STD-881A. (2005). *

* Author bolded certain words in original quote for the purpose of this book.

Given that you only provide a high-level WBS to the project contractors, you don't restrict their ability to properly execute the work. **Allow your contractors the freedom to use the approach that work best for them**, and they'll deliver the work that you need. When managing procurements, providing a high-level WBS to contractors facilitates the Request for Proposals (RFP) responses evaluation with potential vendors.

> The breakdown for WBS components that will be executed by a provider will be decomposed by the provider in the provider's WBS.

HOW DO YOU USE THE WBS IN A BUY-DECISION?

When you acquire deliverables from external vendors, this is called a **buy-decision**. Depending on different project factors like deliverable risk, organization knowledge to create the work, budget, or timelines, one option could work better than the other: make or buy.

When using a buy-decision, you need to define what the deliverable work involved is. To help you visualize the work involved in a buy-decision, Figure 10.6 illustrates the WBS I used for a project for which we outsourced a Web conferencing system. Next to the WBS components, I describe the associated deliverables as defined in the WBS dictionary. You could use a WBS section similar to 1.2.3.1 because all procurements will have a statement of work (SOW), they may have a solutions research, you may need to use a SOW template, you'll obtain the list of potential vendors, will have an outcome as a result of the request for proposals, you'll have a final evaluation of the proposals and a selection of the final vendor, and you'll sign a contract. The process will finish after you issue an executive summary of the procurement for the decision makers, you communicate the final decision to potential vendors, and finally you start working on integrating the acquired deliverable into your project.

1. VIRTUAL OFFICE PROJECT
1.1 Corporate Website
1.2 Project Management
1.2.1 Risks
1.2.2 Costs
1.2.3 Procurements

1.2.3.1 Web Conferencing Procurement

    1.2.3.1.1 Statement of Work (SOW) team

        DELIVERABLE: Approved document with definition of people who will work on this procurement

    1.2.3.2 Solutions Research

        DELIVERABLE: Document with research results of web conferencing solutions in the market

        1.2.3.2.1 Adobe Acrobat Connect Study

        1.2.3.2.2 WebEx Study

        1.2.3.2.3 Live Meeting Study

        1.2.3.2.4 Research Summary

    1.2.3.3 SOW Template

        DELIVERABLE: SOW template approved for this procurement

    1.2.3.4 SOW

        DELIVERABLE: Web conferencing SOW document approved

    1.2.3.5 Potential Vendor List

        DELIVERABLE: List of Potential Vendors

    1.2.3.6 Request For Proposals (RFP)

        DELIVERABLE: Communication letter with RFP to potential vendors

    1.2.3.7 Demostrations and Vendors Responses Evaluation

        DELIVERABLE: Solution Demos. Evaluation sheets complete and rated

    1.2.3.8 Vendor Selection

        DELIVERABLE: Vendor selection decision documented and approved

    1.2.3.9 Contract

        DELIVERABLE: Negotiated contract signed and payment made

    1.2.3.10 Procurement Executive Summary

        DELIVERABLE: Document with summary of the procurement for stakeholders and future records

    1.2.3.11 Web Conferencing System Launch

        DELIVERABLE: Web conferencing system running in production and users trained

1.2.3.2 Teleconferencing Procurement

1.2.3.3 Video Conferencing Procurement

Figure 10.6 WBS section for a buy-decision in a procurement process

WHAT'S THE RELATIONSHIP BETWEEN THE PROJECT WBS AND THE CONTRACT WBS?

Why don't you have to decompose the components that you'll buy? Because you won't manage the work packages associated with them. Since you'll buy them, you don't need to break them down. You'll just break down a few high levels in the WBS until you can communicate the components needed.

There's a structure called the **Contract WBS** (CWBS) which **shows the deliverables that contractors are responsible for.** It has some elements from the overall project WBS. There's one Contract WBS per contract. As a result, if there is a project with several subprojects or deliverables being contracted, then there will be several Contract WBSs. A preliminary version of the Contract WBS will be included in the RFP where potential providers will be requested to extend the Contract WBS to define the total contract scope based on their approach. Providers could suggest modifications, enhancements, or a different, more effective approach based on their experience. The CWBS is also used for reporting and coordinating purposes. Figure 10.7 shows the relationship between the WBS and one or more Contract WBS.

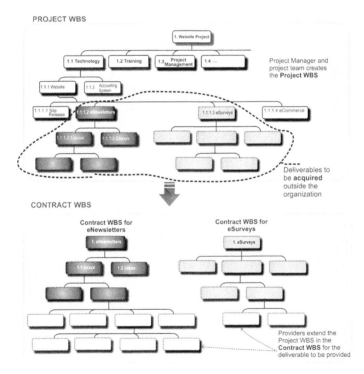

Figure 10.7 Project and Contract WBS relationship

Figure 10.7 shows a couple of things. First, it shows the WBS for the Website Project. There are two deliverables in that project that will be acquired, not made in-house—1.1.1.2 eNewsletters and 1.1.1.3 eSurveys. The project manager with the team will create the WBS shown in the rectangle at the top (labeled Project WBS). For those deliverables that will be acquired (eNewsletters and eSurveys), the project manager decomposes only up to Level 3 of them (which is Level 4-6 in the Project WBS). The project may have Provider A to provide the eNewsletters and Provider B to provide the eSurveys. The project manager will talk with each provider and will give them only the section of the project WBS corresponding to their deliverables. Then each provider will take that information and extend the Contract WBS to further refine the deliverable they have to build. They will further break down the Contract WBS to the appropriate level where they can manage the subcontracted work. This is shown in the rectangle at the bottom (labeled Contract WBS).

Note that in the eNewsletter component, the WBS ID is 1.1.1.2 in the project WBS rectangle at the top. However, the same component in the Contract WBS rectangle at the bottom has a different WBS ID, which is 1. Why? Because **the component could have any WBS ID in the project WBS, but in the contract WBS will always start at Level 1.** This is because for the provider this is the first level to work on.

In chapter 11 I'll discuss the WBS and procurements in global and virtual projects.

HOW DO YOU USE THE WBS IN HUMAN RESOURCES?

When talking about the WBS and its relationship with human resources, there are a couple of things to consider. First, the WBS can help you determine the resources needed for the project deliverables in scope. Secondly, it facilitates the work assignment and explanation to the team members. This section addresses:

* How do you assign work with the WBS?
* How do you use the WBS with the Responsibility Assignment Matrix?

HOW DO YOU ASSIGN WORK WITH THE WBS?

I briefly addressed element owners and work assignments when discussing the WBS fields or attributes in chapter 5, however, there are a few important considerations to stress while getting deeper in human resources management.

First, in a WBS work can be assigned at different levels. Work can be the responsibility of internal or external stakeholders. When it's the responsibility of internal stakeholders and the work will be done in-house, you can use the **WBS as a checklist to ensure that all the components get assigned to the appropriate person**.

A good definition of scope—in the WBS—allows you to better match the skills needed with the work to be delivered. The person that will ultimately achieve the deliverable is added to the WBS element. To add the human resources to your WBS, insert an attribute called "Responsible" or "Owner" as shown in Figure 10.8.

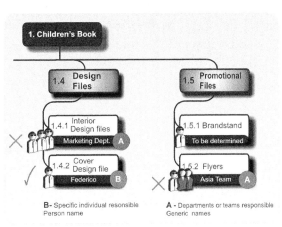

Figure 10.8 Type of WBS elements owners

Second, when adding human resources to the WBS, **be specific. Add the name of a person, not the name of a team or a department**. Why? Because **you need a single person accountable** to each WBS element. When you assign it to a group or a generic name, it's harder to hold someone accountable for the work if problems arise or deadlines are missed. This is especially important for the work packages.

While developing the WBS, you may not know which persons will be responsible for which deliverables. Perhaps the project resources aren't allocated yet. If this is the case, start inserting human resources with generic, or group names when creating the WBS. Once you are

> **practical tip**
>
> *Whenever possible, assign a single person per WBS element instead of a group of individuals.*

able to assign the work and determine the individual who will be responsible for each component, you'll update the WBS by adding their name to it.

Figure 10.8 also shows two components assigned to the Marketing Department and the Asia Team in the WBS. When several members of a team will be involved with completing a deliverable, you can insert the name of the person who leads the group. You could also insert the person within the team or department who will ultimately be responsible for the deliverable.

Third, where the WBS helps you determine the most appropriate source for a specific work package, **the WBS dictionary helps explain the work being assigned**. The WBS dictionary provides additional, valuable information to clarify the scope under assignment. This helps to minimize misunderstandings around what the people responsible need to accomplish.

Finally, the WBS **helps develop the human resource plan**. The human resource plan lists the resources, skills, level of experience, and knowledge needed to complete a work package. The information in the WBS and WBS dictionary help you determine the profile of the human resources that you need to contract or hire. It also aids in determining the resources that need to be negotiated internally so they can join the project team.

HOW DO YOU USE THE WBS WITH THE RESPONSIBILITY ASSIGNMENT MATRIX (RAM)?

I showed you an Organizational Breakdown Structure (OBS) in chapter 3 and explained the difference between it and the WBS. The OBS shows the project organization, the reporting relationships, and the chain of command. **The OBS can also be used in conjunction with the WBS** through the Responsibility Assignment Matrix (RAM). *"[The WBS] supports documentation of the accountability and responsibility for the various deliverables by having a direct relationship among the WBS elements related to the OBS identified through the Responsibility Assignment Matrix (RAM)."*[6]

---

6 *Practice Standard for WBS*—Second Edition. 7. Author bolded certain words in original quote for the purpose of this book.

The **RAM shows and documents the connection between WBS work packages and team members** (Table 10.3).

RESPONSIBILITY ASSIGNMENT MATRIX (RAM)						
Per-son	Role	1.5.2 Master Plan	1.1 Site Content	1.6 System Manuals	1.2 Training	1.3.1 Software Release
Tom	Sponsor	Approver	Approver		Participates	Approver
Luis	Project Manager	Responsible	Approver	Approver	Approver	Approver
Fred	Writer	Input Required		Responsible	Responsible	Reviewer
Lilian	Tech Leader	Input Required	Reviewer	Approver	Participates	Approver
Sayed	Business Analyst	Input Required	Reviewer	Reviewer	Participates	Reviewer
Frank	Developer	Informed	Informed		Responsible	

Table 10.3 RAM integrated with the WBS

In this table the team members are in the first column, and the work packages are in the second row. Examples of work packages are 1.5.2 Master Plan and 1.6 System Manuals. A high-level RAM shows what group or department is responsible for each deliverable. A low-level RAM shows roles, responsibilities, and authority per work package. The numbers showing before the work packages are the WBS IDs from the WBS.

> **practical tip**
>
> *When you use a RAM, you can see all the work packages associated to a person or group, and all the people or groups working on each deliverable.*

One of the most known RAM formats is called **R**esponsible, **A**ccountable, **C**onsult, and **I**nform (**RACI**). These could be the different designations you give to a person when linking him or her to the deliverables. For example, a person who is responsible for a deliverable could be consulted to obtain his or her input when creating the deliverable, or could be merely informed about the deliverable once the work is being executed. The person won't work in the achievement of the deliverable, but must be informed regarding its status.

The RAM ensures a clear understanding of roles and responsibilities in a project team and helps to avoid potential team conflicts. It's good to define the project's RAM as early as possible in the project, preferably once the team was defined, to clarify responsibilities.

In Table 10.3, WBS IDs are not in the same order found in the WBS. You can order the deliverables the way that works best for you when assigning work. In Table 10.3, the Person column contains names of individuals; however, you could use divisions, departments, units, or teams assigned around WBS elements instead. An alternative way of representing a RAM could be a WBS outline in the left columns, and the roles as a row on top.

HOW CAN YOU USE THE WBS IN QUALITY MANAGEMENT?

The same way the scope baseline is an input to manage the project time, cost, risk, and procurement, it's also an input to plan the project's and product's quality. The WBS dictionary generally has information that is important to consider when managing quality. This information can include technical details, quality metrics, performance objectives, or compliance with quality standards, to name a few. Additionally, more details about the quality could be available in the product scope description. Just like you can color code risky WBS components, you can also highlight those deliverables in the WBS where you might have risks associated with quality. You can also use the WBS to communicate quality-related information, or you can link the WBS with different types of quality reports to determine if you have certain deliverables with more quality issues, or those that are defect-free.

The WBS can be used as a tool to report status about quality assurance and quality control. There are many reports related to quality information. Among these reports are quality status, errors, bugs, low levels of performance, and testing results. You could report the quantity of errors found in a group of deliverables, the quality status per deliverables, the list of quality problems per deliverable, the quality test cases per deliverable or the total issues per severity (major, minor, critical) per deliverables. Table 10.4 provides one example of quality reporting presenting the number of internal and external errors, as well as number of error fixed per deliverable. This sample report is linked to the WBS through the associated WBS ID.

ERRORS SUMMARY - bg PROJECT QUALITY REPORT						
WBS ID	Deliverable Name	Internal Errors	External Errors	Fixed Errors	Responsible	Status
1.3.1.1	User Manual	15	0	14	Tom	Pending
1.3.1.2	Administrator Manual	5	0	15	Tom	Approved
1.3.1.3	On-line help	12	4	16	Tom	Approved
1.4.1.1	Release ver. 1	36	0	13	Linda	Pending
1.4.1.2	Release ver. 2	0	0	0	Linda	Pending
1.2.2.1	Spanish flyer	18	1	17	Judy	Approved
1.2.2.2	English flyer	21	2	0	Judy	Pending

Table 10.4 Errors summary per major deliverables with link to WBS

Even though properly managing the project quality is a key success factor for any project, there is limited interaction between the quality area and the WBS. Quality reporting is the aspect that I found more interesting about linking the project quality with the project or product scope. By linking the WBS with quality reports, you gain a richer understanding of the deliverables, quality and you can communicate quality issues and quality performance-related information or metrics. The project WBS can be used to report quality information and frequently the product WBS is used and linked to the project quality.

HOW CAN YOU USE THE WBS IN STAKEHOLDER MANAGEMENT?

One of the key concerns of stakeholders is the project or product scope, as well as the impacts of scope changes on them. In addition, stakeholders are key in providing input to the creation and validation of the WBS. This is why scope management is also related to stakeholder management. Throughout this book I talk about stakeholders, so here I will just add a few things specifically about the link between these two areas.

First, the stakeholder register often indicates the scope that each stakeholder is most interested in or concerned about, and the impact of change to them. Whenever you analyze a scope change request, one of the things you do is to determine how the scope change would impact stakeholders.

Second, as a result of controlling stakeholder engagement process, you could need to issue a scope change request; and that would demand an update in the WBS.

Third, stakeholders need to be notified when scope modifications arise or scope approvals are made. We have talked already in this chapter about the relationship between communications and the WBS, and this also applies to stakeholders.

Finally, when you assign the person responsible for a WBS component, that person could be any stakeholder, not only a project team member. So there you have another relationship between the WBS and stakeholders.

This concludes a chapter with one of the most practical approaches to manage the different areas in a project and how they all relate to the scope management and the effective use of the WBS. There's a powerful benefit in the integration of the WBS with all the project management areas of knowledge as I have demonstrated. In the next chapter, I will present some considerations and tips regarding using the WBS in the context of managing global or virtual projects.

chapter 11

How Do You Use the WBS in Global and Virtual Projects?

We need to be prepared to suceed in our diverse and interconnected world.

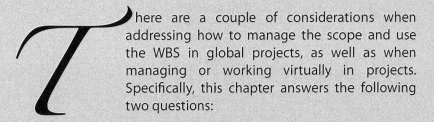here are a couple of considerations when addressing how to manage the scope and use the WBS in global projects, as well as when managing or working virtually in projects. Specifically, this chapter answers the following two questions:

- How do you identify global characteristics in a WBS?
- How do you use the WBS in global and virtual projects?

HOW DO YOU IDENTIFY GLOBAL CHARACTERISTICS IN A WBS?

In a project that spans multiple regions of the world, in some cases you may need to **highlight in the WBS which pieces of work are executed in different locations**. For example, part of a project team could be in Latin America, part in North America, and a sub-team can be based in Asia. All of the teams report to the same project manager based in Latin America. It may be easier for the purpose of discussing and communicating the scope to identify the components that each group will be responsible for, and which ones will be executed in conjunction. In a WBS, you may have at least two options for highlighting the regions of the world in which the deliverables will be met:

1. Using a different color or a flag, (Figure 11.1) for the components in the United States, Brazil, Uruguay, and China, or
2. Using an attribute in the WBS and/or WBS dictionary to indicate which country corresponds to each WBS component.

You can use different colors for the different countries or regions where the components will be executed, or you can use icons, bitmaps, or flags for this purpose in global projects.

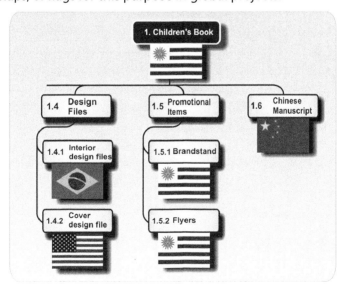

Figure 11.1 Use of colors and flags for global WBS components

Figure 11.1 shows the use of country flags involved in the Book project in which the project manager oversees the project virtually from Uruguay but the graphic designers are located in Brazil and in United States. The Brazilian designer works on component 1.4.1 Interior Design files for the book, while the United States designer works on component 1.4.2 Cover design file. The Chinese manuscript is published in China and the book's promotional items are executed in Uruguay.

When I have different teams or people working either virtually or on-site in different parts of the world, I use the flags as a visual representation. Some of the software reviewed in chapter 7 allows you to insert icons and images in WBS components. For example, in MindView®, you can easily insert bitmaps or pre-defined images through its multimedia catalog.

WHAT DO YOU CONSIDER IN THE WBS IN GLOBAL AND VIRTUAL PROJECTS?

The same concept discussed about identifying the location for a global project in the WBS can apply to identify other characteristics such as the language, time zone, or country associated with each component. Why this is important? Because if you have sessions to create the WBS with the different teams and they are working from different time zones, or they speak different languages, you may need to define the strategies to follow and the options that you have to create, validate, communicate, and maintain the WBS. You need to plan how you'll work with a distributed team to make sure they provide input and are part of the WBS creation process.

Also, additional work may be needed to manage global and/or virtual teams. For example, if you have a project that includes teams from China and the Brazil, and the Brazilian team has never worked in China or with members from that part of the world, it would be important for them to receive training on what would be the best approach to work with teammates from China. Brazilian team members would benefit from knowing about Chinese culture, including their expectations of peers, what is normal behavior for them, and how they approach work. The Chinese teammates would also benefit from knowing these things about their Brazilian counterparts. Team norms are very important in virtual teams. Thus, you would **include**

additional WBS components related to training and management to address distributed or virtual teams, especially if this is the first time you are managing a multicultural and/or virtual project. The WBS should also cover additional components if the project requires:

- 24x7 coverage (24 hours a day, seven days a week) to different time zones and languages,
- travel for face-to-face meetings, and
- project budget presented in different **currencies**. In this case, if you show costs in the WBS, you'll need to use more than one cost field.

There are other considerations associated to global projects like **political or regulatory** that may impact the scope. For example, if you always managed projects in your country, and this is the first time you'll do it in another country with different government regulations, you may need to **add WBS components to consider the work related to learn about those regulations** and the work needed in this new scenario.

When part of or the team will work remotely, there is work related to **making sure that the technology needed to work virtually is in place**. This is the technology to facilitate teleconferencing, video conferencing, web conferencing, chats, wikis, or devices and systems. Productivity and motivation shouldn't be affected because some or all of the team is working virtually. Unless the project organization already has these systems and devices in place, you may need to **define the technology to use in a virtual environment, to purchase it, to install it, and to train team members and stakeholders in its use**. All of that has work associated with it, and that work should be captured in the WBS. You should not underestimate the technology needed and someone should be responsible for it.

A final thought on this is that in a project with the aforementioned characteristics, you should think what will be the statements of work and contracts that you'll need to effectively manage the project in a new environment, and then consider them when creating the WBS.

Global, multicultural, and virtual projects are growing all over the world. There's an increasing tendency for projects to be executed this way. Project managers need to be ready to work within the boundaries of their own countries as well as overseas. You also need to be ready to and capable of working in the virtual or remote environment as many teams move off-site.

> **practical tip**

To avoid overrunning costs or decreasing performance for assuming that a virtual or global project runs like an on-site or local one, at the beginning of the project, you should identify the work related working virtually or in global projects.

chapter 12

Can You Use the WBS in Agile Projects?

"The WBS is used for the project as a whole while components created with agile methods fit in a Product WBS inside the Project WBS."
- Liliana Buchtik

he title of this chapter is a question I am asked often times in my WBS book workshops. Many people think those two concepts, WBS and Agile, are incompatible, and that is not true. I have used the WBS in projects where part of the project scope was delivered in increments via agile methodologies. The PMBOK Guide says: "The planning for the next iteration is carried out as work progresses on the current iteration's scope and deliverables." This means the PMBOK Guide is not against the use of agile methods and it does consider the possibility to plan and deliver the scope incrementally. I'll discuss this in the next few pages. This chapter is more applicable to the information technology (IT) field.

Why am I talking about agile project management in a WBS book? What is agile project management? I wrote this chapter to present

* *PMBOK® Guide*—Fifth Edition. 45.

a few clarifications and my personal perspective on WBS and agile based on questions I received while delivering conferences or workshops about the *Secrets to Mastering the WBS in Real-World Projects*. I can't end this book without first referring to agile project management. I also think this is appropriate to mention in the context of WBS because there are a series of misunderstandings regarding agile projects and its alignment with the *PMBOK® Guide*, as well as how to manage the scope under those approaches.

I'll define what agile is and a few related concepts before proceeding. If you are familiar with these definitions, you can skip them.

Iterative and incremental development is a way to develop software where you deliver subsets of the system or final product in sequential iterations. The final iteration is the complete product release. Thus your system grows in increments or iterations. *Each* **iteration** *is a self-contained mini-project."* [1]

Agile is a development methodology and framework and a subset of iterative methods. It is based on adaptive planning, it encourages agility, and embraces change. Most of the practices related to agile include adapting and refining plans throughout the development or project.

Agile project management is guided by the principles of the agile manifesto and principles which include individuals and interactions over processes and tools, working software over comprehensive documentation, customer collaboration over contract negotiation, and responding to change over following a plan.[2]

Scrum is one example of agile methods where team members in a self-directed team work in the same room and meet daily in short stand-up meetings to coordinate. I'll use Scrum as an example in this chapter.

It is not the intent of this book to explain in detail what agile is. At the end of the chapter, I provide information for you to further

1   Larman, C. *Agile and Iterative Development: A Manager's Guide.* 9.
2   *Agile and Iterative Development: A Manager's Guide.* 28.

read about it if you are interested. At one of the conferences where I spoke, someone asked me *"Is agile project management a threat to the* PMBOK® Guide? *Where does the WBS fits in agile project management?"* Another attendee said *"The* PMBOK® Guide *doesn't support agile project management and is the old traditional way of managing projects."* I could go on and on about the questions and comments I receive regarding what some call the "heavy, traditional" project management approach versus "light, agile" project management approach.

I disagree that there is one correct way or approach. I believe that a good project manager learns and knows about the various approaches and practices and then chooses what works best for the specific project, organization, or product. **You can gain excellent concepts and techniques from agile as well as from the** *PMBOK®* *Guide*. I have seen projects where both approaches were used in combination, such as projects where a Project Management Professional (PMP)® certified project manager managed the project and a Scrum Master managed the product to be delivered. This is an example using a Scrum Master, which applies to Scrum that is only one of the options to use when managing agile projects.

It's funny sometimes to read blogs or information about those extremists championing for or against agile. **Most project managers either work in one of those worlds—agile—or the other—** *PMBOK® Guide* **framework—but few of them know both or how to use them together for the project's benefit**. There could be projects or programs where some areas could be managed "lighter" than others. For example, I'm familiar with a project which is pretty heavy in its documentation on the business side due to the business' needs. However, software development is using agile methods. Both deliverables belong to the same project. There's only one project manager, but there's also a Scrum Master to manage the software development pieces.

I worked with iterative development for many years. In one of the projects I managed, we were considering starting using agile, we discussed the pros and cons with using it in a software development project. In trying to understand how to better manage the project and what the similarities and differences with *PMBOK® Guide* are, I read books and papers about agile. Unfortunately, it was a challenge to find good literature about the relationship between the *PMBOK® Guide* and agile. Most of the articles I found were written by people who understand agile well, but not the *PMBOK® Guide,* or vice versa. This is why I believe there are misunderstandings and questions in the air, some of which don't make sense.

So let me tell you first what I concluded after some research and I what I believe. Then I'll present some examples and quotes from the *PMBOK® Guide* as well as from a book about iterative, incremental, and agile development to help you gain a better understanding on these approaches and how they can work together.

I believe the following about the *PMBOK® Guide* related to agile. The *PMBOK® Guide*:

- ❀ **Is in alignment with iterative, incremental, and agile development.**
- ❀ **Can't be substituted by agile.** They are two different things and can be used in combination when needed and appropriate. While agile principles are mostly related to software development, the principles in the *PMBOK® Guide* apply to most of the industries, including software development.
- ❀ **Is not a methodology, but it's a framework or guideline.** As such, it can be used to manage the overall project, while the project manager, the technical leader, Scrum Master, or someone else can manage the deliverables associated with software development using an iterative, incremental, or agile approach.
- ❀ **Is as valid and useful as it always was.** The *PMBOK® Guide* is the most globally accepted and recognized framework for most of the projects most of the time, while the application of agile project management is reduced to specific kinds of projects like those of new product development or inventive projects. Agile is mostly known in industries like IT where there is high uncertainty and constant changes. I support agile for certain kind of projects; however, that doesn't mean agile can be used for all projects or all the time.
- ❀ **Recognizes that the project manager delivers the project with the help of a team**.

I'll discuss these bullets more.

PMBOK® GUIDE ALIGNMENT WITH AGILE

The *PMBOK® Guide* is in alignment with iterative, incremental, evolutionary, and agile development. It doesn't say that you have to have 100 percent of the project defined up front and then freeze it from day one. This is a misunderstanding. What's more, the *PMBOK® Guide* has provided guidance for years regarding iterative planning as well as the possibility to request changes through the change control processes. You may say: *"OK Liliana, but that's too formal and we don't need that in agile."* And that's fine. It's probably formal, but not impossible. And the degree of formality depends on the project's needs.

To support my statement, below I list a series of quotes from the *PMBOK® Guide* that show the *PMBOK®*-agile alignment:[3]

> The *PMBOK® Guide* doesn't say you can't process changes and need to freeze everything up front.

* *"Due to the potential for change, the development of the project management plan is an **iterative** activity and is **progressively elaborated** throughout the project's life cycle. Progressive elaboration involves continuously improving and detailing a plan as more-detailed and specific information and more accurate estimates become available. Progressive elaboration allows a project management team to define work and manage it to a greater level of detail as the project evolves."* (p. 6)

* *Rolling Wave Planning is an **iterative planning** technique in which the work to be accomplished in the near term is planned in detail while the work in the future is planned at a higher level. It is a form of progressive elaboration. Therefore, work can exist at various levels of detail depending on where it is in the project life cycle. During early strategic planning, when information is less defined, work packages may be decomposed to the known level of detail. As more is known about the upcoming events in the near term, work packages can be decomposed into activities. (p.152)*

* *"Developing an acceptable project schedule is often an **iterative process**."* (p. 174)

---

3   *PMBOK® Guide*—Fifth Edition. Page numbers as noted in text. Author bolded certain words in original quote for the purpose of this book.

❋ *"Identify Risks is an **iterative process** because new risks may evolve or become known as the project progresses through its life cycle."* (p. 321)

❋ *"**Iterative and incremental** life cycles are ones in which project phases (or iterations) intentionally repeat one or more project activities as the project team's understanding of the product increases. Iterations develop the product through a series of repeated cycles, while increments successively add to the functionality of the product. These life cycles develop the product both iteratively and incrementally. During an iteration, activities from all Project Management Process Groups will be performed. At the end of each iteration, a deliverable or set of deliverables will be completed. Future iterations may enhance those deliverables or create new ones."* (p. 45)

There are more quotes supporting this approach, but this last quote is the perfect fit for agile within the *PMBOK® Guide* framework.

Why wouldn't you plan everything up front and only plan the current phase? **Sometimes, you don't have all the details or information at the early stages**. If you are dealing with a project that has a high level of change, a new product development, or projects like that, it makes sense in that context to use agile. However, in using agile, do you contradict the practices contained within the *PMBOK® Guide*? No. The last quote above is mentioned in a *PMBOK® Guide* section where it discusses the basic types of relationships that can exist among project phases. Those are: sequential, overlapping, predictive, iterative and incremental, and adaptive. Agile fits in the iterative and incremental life cycles. This doesn't mean that all the projects can be done, planned, and executed with agile. There are times when you can and it makes more sense to use a sequential, overlapping, adaptive, or predictive type of relationship instead of an iterative.

The *PMBOK® Guide* says that this progressive detailing of the project management plan is called rolling wave planning, while agile project management says that *"Adaptive planning in IID [iterative and incremental development] methods is a refinement of the well-known rolling wave planning concept."*[4] Thus, both the **PMBOK® Guide and adaptive planning talk about the same concept: rolling wave planning.** This is not to say that agile and the *PMBOK® Guide* are the same. They are not. But agile can fit within the *PMBOK® Guide* and there is no misalignment between them.

---

4   Larman, C. *Agile and Iterative Development: A Manager's Guide.* 253.

THE ROLE OF THE PROJECT MANAGER

Regardless of the approach you use, it's important to note that both are team oriented. I've heard some misconceptions that a project manager working under the *PMBOK® Guide* framework works alone, without much involvement from the project team. This is not correct. A good project manager doesn't work alone. It's impossible to manage and execute a project without working as a team. Agile and Iterative Development: A Manager's Guide says: *"A theme of agile project management in Scrum and XP is the devolution of both control and planning to the entire team, not the manager. The manager does not create a WBS, schedule, or estimates; this is done as a team."*[5] I agree with this and so does the *PMBOK® Guide*.

If you go back to chapter 4, when I discussed who creates the WBS, that was one of the key questions, and I did not say that the project manager does this alone. It's a team effort done with the project team and stakeholders. When the *PMBOK® Guide* mentions tools and techniques for defining the scope, it says that, among other things, brainstorming and expert judgment from the stakeholders and the project team can be used. It also says that *"[The project scope statement] also provides a common understanding of the project scope **among stakeholders**."*[6] It doesn't say that it's the project manager understanding only. The team is part of it as well.

Further, in PMI's *Practice Standard for Scheduling* it says that "... *durations for risk analysis should be made by those who will be performing the activities or by one who has experience performing similar activities."*[7] Who will be performing the activities? The project team. Thus, the project team needs to prepare the estimates, not the project manager alone. The project manager under the *PMBOK® Guide* isn't shown as a dictator or a person that tells people what to do. It's a leader, someone with experience who will work together and coach the team members.

I know the goal of this chapter is to discuss how the WBS and scope management ties into agile project management. However, let me clarify another misunderstanding regarding project documentation in *PMBOK® Guide* and agile. The *PMBOK® Guide* doesn't promote comprehensive documentation just for the sake of documenting.

---

5   Larman, C. *Agile and Iterative Development: A Manager's Guide.*

6   *PMBOK® Guide*—Fifth Edition. 123. Author bolded certain words in original quote for the purpose of this book.

7   *Practice Standard for Scheduling*—Second Edition. 10.

The *PMBOK® Guide* identifies the subset of the project management body of knowledge generally recognized as good practice. *"Good practice does not mean the knowledge described should always be applied uniformly to all projects; **the organization and/or or project management team is responsible for determining what is appropriate for any given project.**"*[8] This means that according to the project's needs, in your scope management plan you may decide that you only need a high-level WBS or a detailed one. The *PMBOK® Guide* provides further guidelines for this in the following statement. *"The scope management plan may be **formal or informal, highly detailed, or broadly framed, based upon the needs** of the project."*[9] For instance, this also means that according to the project's needs, in your scope management plan you may decide that you only need a high-level WBS or a detailed one.

Depending on project's needs, you may also want to use agile, for example by using Scrum that uses something called the "feature backlog" to track and prioritize requirements and to define and manage the scope.

> **It isn't the intention of the PMBOK® Guide to promote heavy documentation.**

Throughout the standard, the key is to follow good practices that are based on the project needs. Each project is different. For example, I worked for four years in the government in especially big and multi-year projects. When doing so there was heavy documentation, and for those projects it made sense. I also worked in private companies or organizations where that same load of documentation was not valuable and we just adapted to the project's needs. If you have a project to deliver a new plane, or an important construction project, I bet you can't avoid documenting. I met the project manager of *Rio 2016,* a project to host the Olympics and Paralympics, a multi-year project that may change many factors in Rio de Janeiro, Brazil. It involves education, construction, marketing, promotion, software, and more. It's an incredible project. What could they use in this project? *PMBOK® Guide* framework? Agile? Or both?

---

8   *PMBOK® Guide*—Fifth Edition. 2. Author bolded certain words in original quote for the purpose of this book.
9   *PMBOK® Guide*—Fifth Edition. 110. Author bolded certain words in original quote for the purpose of this book.

WHY AGILE WON'T REPLACE THE *PMBOK® GUIDE*?

I believe that this won't happen. Why? Simple. As presented above, agile and the *PMBOK® Guide* aren't mutually exclusive. **The PMBOK® Guide goes beyond agile project management and addresses techniques that are needed to manage a project as a whole**. Such concepts and techniques are not discussed under agile. For example, your project calls for a system component valued at $150 million and your customer, the government, requires you to receive a request for proposal. Does the agile method provide guidance on that? No. The *PMBOK® Guide* does. Am I saying that *PMBOK® Guide* is better? No. It's different. I support *PMBOK® Guide* 100 percent and I also use agile for development work if the conditions are appropriate.

The *PMBOK® Guide* addresses more of how to deal with the **project scope**, while agile, in general, is more concerned with how to deal with the **product scope** (software development scope). That you may probably have a project using *PMBOK® Guide* framework in combination with agile, and you'll need a WBS for the overall project, but you may decide not to have a Product WBS for the product scope.

PMBOK® Guide	--> PROJECT Scope
Agile	--> PRODUCT Scope

You can manage the product scope based on any iterative approach. I understand iterative, incremental, evolutionary, adaptive, and agile are not the same, I'm using those terms indistinctly in this chapter as conceptually any of them are valid for this discussion.

TRADITIONAL VERSUS AGILE

Can I talk about "traditional project management" versus "agile project management"? No. Can I say that the *PMBOK® Guide* framework doesn't support agile project management and is the old, traditional way of managing projects? No. You can **use the *PMBOK® Guide* as your framework to manage most of the projects most of the time, and then combine it and use it with the methodology or tools of your preference** (prototyping,

Scrum, waterfall, and others).

While the *PMBOK® Guide* is an established framework, agile project management has been applied mostly in the IT industry and there are projects and industries with projects that couldn't be implemented with agile. I have been working in the IT field for years and most of the time, while I worked as a programmer and system analyst I worked using iterative development and prototyping. However, that was the way I managed the software development piece of the work, not the entire project.

You could manage the project as a whole and then use agile to manage software development. You'll have WBS for your entire project, and you may or not may need to have a WBS for your software product.

PMBOK® Guide has many tools and techniques that can help a project manager to manage agile projects. For example, under the Communications Management area, it addresses how to identify stakeholders. It also provide guides and ideas on how to deliver information and manage stakeholder's expectations, how to distribute information, to name a few.

WBS AND SCOPE IN AGILE PROJECTS

What is the difference between these two approaches? The major difference is how you manage the project scope, how you manage the product scope, and as such, the way you create the WBS in such projects.

In managing a project as a whole, you go beyond the discussion of what features and functions you'll have in the next iteration or release, you plan and manage all the needed project management areas. If you use *PMBOK® Guide*, in your WBS you'll certainly not only have the technology deliverables, but also other deliverables from other areas outside software. If you use agile with *PMBOK® Guide*, the section of the WBS for the technology work will be at a high level at first, but you'll detail it as you gain more information and as the next phases and iterations are planned. You'll have a high-level product scope in the WBS and the details will come every couple of weeks for each iteration. Depending on the approach you use, you may not need to add the product WBS; you just add a software package in the WBS with no decomposition.

Also, note that many times in software projects you don't have the conditions or you can't create them to work with agile. In one of the most critical projects I managed a couple of years ago while working in the Department of Justice of my country, the law had set a date to start using a new mechanism to identify the judicial files all across the country and across all the jurisdictional offices and tribunals. That was not something we could negotiate with the customer. Our customers were thousands of users dispersed throughout the country, and the law had set the date. I had to plan and execute a program composed of 13 software projects to impact 13 information systems in the government offices and there was no room for failure. We had to release all those projects at the same time. They all had to have the same quantity of features they had before the new mechanisms became operational. There was no room for iterations.

So even if you sometimes can use agile, as a project manager, you need to be prepared to work according to the *PMBOK® Guide*. On the other hand, **you also need to be open and flexible to adapt and learn other methods** like agile so you can use them when it's best for your project.

Everyone likes agility. And project managers are all often under the pressure of deadlines. It's not the point to talk against agile or the *PMBOK® Guide*. **It's time to learn the best things from both approaches and use them for the benefit of the project and to deliver great results.** Even though I consider myself a specialist in the *PMBOK® Guide*, I don't consider myself an expert in agile. I have worked for years with iterative development and participated in agile projects. However, I'm always looking to become a better project manager and

> **practical tip**
>
> *The WBS is not used in agile, but if you use PMBOK® Guide for the overall project, and you want to represent in the WBS your technology deliverables that use agile, then instead of defining 100 percent of the software development work, you decompose only the work for the next iteration, and keep the other technology deliverables at a very high level.*

apply as many tools and techniques as I can to positively impact the projects I manage. I hope to have provided light to some misunderstandings and examples of similarities and differences as a base to discuss scope management and WBS with agile and *PMBOK® Guide*.

If you are interested in learning more about agile you can reach out to the Scrum Alliance[10]. If you are interested in learning more about both the *PMBOK® Guide* and agile together, you can reach out to the Project Management Institute (PMI)[11]. PMI has a group of members and PMP® certified project managers interested in agile that constitute the PMI Agile Community of Practice.

---

10   Online at www.scrumalliance.org.
11   Online at www.pmi.org.

Conclusion

"We all have reasons for not doing what we ought to do."
John Maxwell[1]

J want to finish this book with a request to you. Please consider the WBS as a valuable tool especially if you haven't tried to use it. Give it a try, just once or twice. If you have tried it before, try it again and this time, apply the concepts, tips, and suggestions found in this book. Then share with me the results. There shouldn't be any excuses not to use the WBS because it really has the power to help you improve your project planning and execution.

I've done my part. I've shared with you all I gathered from years of experience working on projects and discussing projects and the WBS globally with project managers, students, and consultants. Now, it's your turn to put this into practice. You have here the *Secrets to Mastering the WBS in Real-World Projects*. Start applying them today and making a positive impact in your project and business results.

---

1   Maxwell, J. 2007. *Talent is never enough*. Nashville, TN: Thomas Nelson, Inc. (Spanish version)

Some people say: *"we never use the WBS here," "we don't have the culture to use it in our projects".* My suggestion for you as a project manager is to **preach by example**. If some project managers don't use the WBS, it's probably a result of not having seen its value and its benefits. Oftentimes, they don't know how to use it successfully in real-world projects. They probably know about it in theory, but not in practice. The WBS is in your hands to show its value by mastering it. I have worked as a project manager in some organizations where most of the project managers wouldn't use a WBS and as a result, the stakeholders weren't accustomed to it at all. Since my first projects working with those same stakeholders I used the WBS and they immediately saw the value in it and learned to rely on it.

You may say: *"Okay, Liliana, I read it all, how do I get to master the WBS immediately?"* And the answer is: ***"Use the WBS."***

...USE THE WBS... USE THE WBS... USE THE WBS!

I've talked several times in this book about reasons for project failure, and one of the top ten reasons for failure is that project managers don't use methods or the methods they use are not appropriate.[1] So I encourage you to use it he WBS.

There's no way to master anything without trying it in practice. Start using it now in every project. Now that you have the foundations and ideas from this book, you'll learn by experimenting. You'll discover new things as you mature in its use and in each project you'll find it more valuable. Learning and results come with practice. We can't win a championship without preparation, training, and practice. The same thing applies to succeed as a project manager, and to use the WBS successfully. We need preparation and experimentation. Spend some time to learn and try it today to avoid delays, issues, and negative impacts tomorrow.

It'll take some time at the beginning with your team to define the WBS, but it's a great investment of your time. Believe me, it's worth it. The next time you start a project, gather your team initially and then your stakeholders, and discuss with them the use and benefits of the WBS for the project. You can prepare a presentation for them about the WBS and how your team can better manage the scope, as well as the positive impact on the project planning and on risk

---

1   Project Management Institute. December 2003. PM Network. PA: USA. Project Management Institute

management. Start defining the WBS from the very beginning with the stakeholders. Make sure that the key stakeholders are involved, as discussed in chapter 2, and that all of them understand the scope of work and how the work will be delivered, communicated, and measured.

Your first WBS won't be perfect and won't make sense in some of its areas, but as you keep using it, learning about it, and testing different approaches, you'll become comfortable with it. Little by little, it will make a positive impact in your projects. Remember John Maxwell's words: *"We all have reasons for not doing what we ought to do."* I truly hope that after reading this book you can't find reasons **not** to enhance your scope management by using the WBS. Remember what Aristotle said: *"We are what we repeatedly do. Excellence then, is not an act, but a habit."*

The US President, Thomas Jefferson, said:
> *"I find that the harder I work,*
> *the more luck I seem to have"*[2].

Like him, I say:
> *"I find that the more I correctly use the WBS,*
> *the more luck I seem to have* managing projects succesfully"

> **Start improving your projects**
> **by mastering the WBS today!**

Feel free to send me your beneficial comments with suggestions, additions, deletions, and any example that you would like to share which I may use in future editions of this book.

Go to www.buchtik.com to provide me with your valuable feedback.

---

2   ThinkExist. http://thinkexist.com/quotation/i_find_that_the_harder_i_work-the_more_luck_i/176331.html (accessed October 2009)

Appendices

Abbreviations and Acronyms

References and Resources

About the Author

Applying the WBS

Appendix I
Project Management Element Decomposition

Below are simplified WBS elements representing the project management work in a project.

WBS ID	WBS Component Name
1	Project Management
1.1	Integration Management
1.1.1	Project Charter
1.1.2	Kickoff Meeting Presentation
1.1.3	Project Management Plan
1.1.4	Other Plans (Deployment Plan, Release Plan, etc., as needed)
1.1.5	Configuration Management
1.1.5.1	Change Control Process Document
1.1.5.2	Change Request Templates
1.1.5.3	Change Requests
1.1.6	Work Performance Measurements
1.1.7	Lessons Learned

1.2	**Scope Management**	
1.2.1	Requirements	
1.2.1.1	Requirements Document	
1.2.1.2	Requirements Traceability Matrix	
1.2.1.3	Use Case Documents	
1.2.1.4	Requirements Management Plan	
1.2.1.5	Feature Backlog (if applicable)	
1.2.2	Scope Baseline	
1.2.2.1	Scope Statement Document	
1.2.2.2	WBS	
1.2.2.3	WBS Dictionary	
1.2.3	Deliverable Acceptance Documents	
1.3	**Time Management**	
1.3.1	Project Schedule	
1.3.1.1	Master Schedule	
1.3.1.2	Other Schedules (Technical, Quality, etc.)	
1.3.2	Project Milestone Chart	
1.4	**Cost Management**	
1.4.1	Cost Estimates	
1.4.2	Basis of Estimates	
1.4.3	Project Budget	
1.4.4	Budget Forecast	
1.4.5	Cost Performance Baseline	
1.4.6	Project Funding Requirements	
1.4.7	Quotes	
1.5	**Quality Management**	
1.5.1	Quality Management Plan	
1.5.2	Quality Metrics	
1.5.3	Quality Checklists	
1.5.4	Quality Control Measurements	
1.5.5	Quality Assurance Testing Plan	
1.5.6	Quality Assurance Testing Records	
1.5.7	User Acceptance Testing Plan	
1.5.8	User Acceptance Testing Records	
1.5.9	Bugs and Defects Tracking	
1.6	Human Resource Management	

1.6.1	Human Resource Plan
1.6.2	Positions Descriptions
1.6.3	Responsibility Assignment Matrix
1.6.4	Resource Calendars
1.6.5	Team Contact List
1.6.6	Team Norms Document
1.6.7	Team Training Plan
1.6.8	Team Performance Assessments
1.7	**Communications Management**
1.7.1	Organizational Breakdown Structure
1.7.2	Communications Plan
1.7.3	Project Reviews
1.7.4	Project Reports
1.7.5	Meeting Agendas and Minutes
1.8	**Risk Management**
1.8.1	Risk Management Plan
1.8.2	Risk Registry
1.8.3	Risk Breakdown Structure
1.8.4	Issue Registry
1.8.5	Risk Meeting Minutes
1.9	**Procurement Management**
1.9.1	Acquisitions Plan
1.9.2	Make-or-Buy Decisions
1.9.3	Source Selection Criteria
1.9.4	Firms Evaluation Forms
1.9.5	RFP Templates
1.9.6	Contracts and SOWs
1.9.7	Confidentiality Agreement Forms
1.9.8	Purchase Orders
1.10	**Stakeholder Management**
1.10.1	Stakeholder Register
1.10.2	Stakeholder Management Plan
1.10.3	Power/Interest Grid, Power/Influence Grid, Influence/Impact Grid, Salience Model
1.10.4	Stakeholder Assessment Engagement Matrix

Appendix II
Generic WBS Template

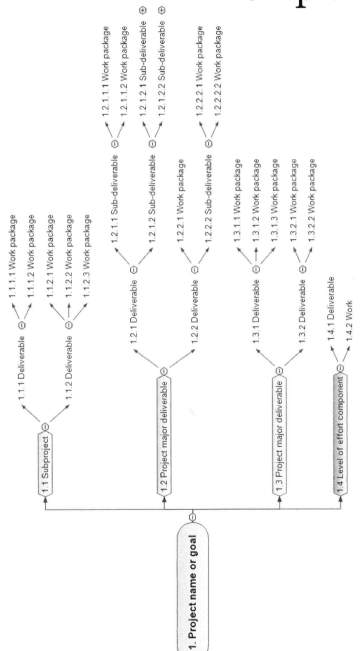

Appendix III
Real-World WBS Examples

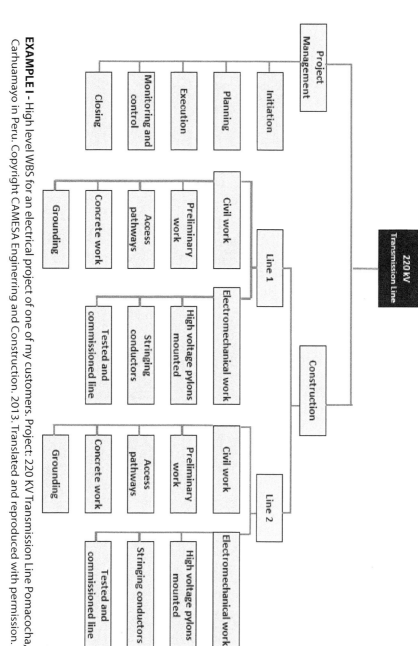

EXAMPLE I - High level WBS for an electrical project of one of my customers. Project: 220 KV Transmission Line Pomacocha, Carhuamayo in Peru. Copyright CAMESA Enginerring and Construction. 2013. Translated and reproduced with permission.

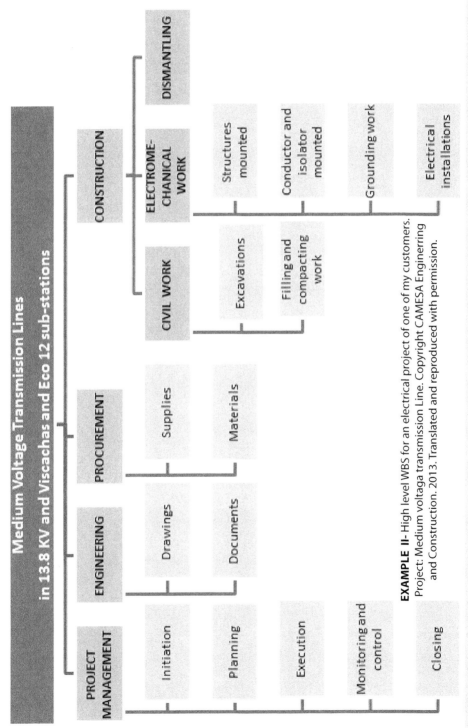

EXAMPLE II- High level WBS for an electrical project of one of my customers. Project: Medium voltaga transmission Line. Copyright CAMESA Enginerring and Construction. 2013. Translated and reproduced with permission.

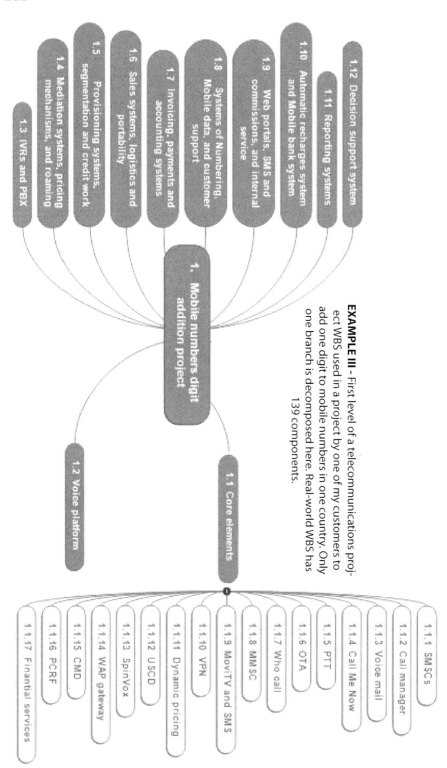

EXAMPLE III - First level of a telecommunications project WBS used in a project by one of my customers to add one digit to mobile numbers in one country. Only one branch is decomposed here. Real-world WBS has 139 components.

1. Mobile numbers digit addition project

1.1 Core elements

1.2 Voice platform

1.3 IVRs and PBX

1.4 Mediation systems, pricing mechanisms, and roaming

1.5 Provisioning systems, segmentation and credit work

1.6 Sales systems, logistics and portability

1.7 Invoicing, payments and accounting systems

1.8 Systems of Numbering, Mobile data, and customer support

1.9 Web portals, SMS and commissions, and internal service

1.10 Automatic recharges system and Mobile bank system

1.11 Reporting systems

1.12 Decision support system

1.1.1 SMSCs

1.1.2 Call manager

1.1.3 Voice mail

1.1.4 Call Me Now

1.1.5 PTT

1.1.6 OTA

1.1.7 Who call

1.1.8 MMSC

1.1.9 MoviTV and SMS

1.1.10 VPN

1.1.11 Dynamic pricing

1.1.12 USCD

1.1.13 SpinVox

1.1.14 WAP gateway

1.1.15 CMD

1.1.16 PCRF

1.1.17 Finantial services

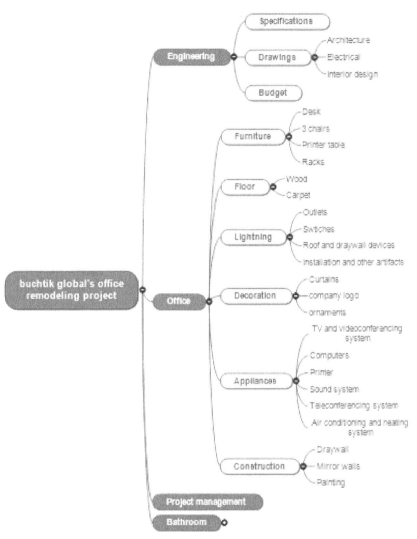

EXAMPLE IV- WBS for an architecture/construction project. Buchtik global's office remodelation

Abbreviations and Acronyms

Bg®	Buchtik Global
BOM	Bill of Materials
CBS	Contract Breakdown Structure
CBS	Cost Breakdown Structure
CEO	Chief Executive Officer
CWBS	Contract Work Breakdown Structure. See CBS
DoD	U.S. Department of Defense
FIN	Finance
HTML	Hypertext Markup Language
IID	Iterative and Incremental Development
ID	Identification
IEEE	Institute of Electrical and Electronics Engineers
IT	Information Technology
MIL-STD	Military Standard
MKT	Marketing
OBS	Organizational Breakdown Structure
PhD	Doctor of Philosophy
***PMBOK*®**	A Guide to the Project Management Body of Knowledge
PMI	Project Management Institute Inc.
PMO	Project Management Office
PMP®	Project Management Professional
RACI	Responsible, Accountable, Consult, Inform
RAM	Responsibility Assignment Matrix
RBS	Risk Breakdown Structure
RBS	Resource Breakdown Structure
RFP	Request for Proposal
VSD	Visio Drawing
WBS	Work Breakdown Structure
WP	Work Package

References and Resources

Department of Defense. 1993. *Department of Defense Handbook: Work Breakdown Structures for Defense Materiel Items*, MIL-HDBK-881A and MIL-STD-881B, Washington D.C.

Department of Defense. 2005. *Department of Defense Handbook: Work Breakdown Structures for Defense Materiel Items*, MIL-HDBK-881A and MIL-STD-881A, Washington D.C.

Evrard, E., and Nieto, A. 2004. *Boosting business performance through program and project management.* Belgium. PriceWaterhouseCoopers.

Gladwell, M. 2008. *Outliers*. New York: Little Brown.

Haugan, G. 2003. *The Work Breakdown Structure in Government Contracting.* Vienna, VA: Management Concepts.

Institute of Electrical and Electronics Engineers (IEEE). 1997. IEEE/EIA 12207 Development Process Work Breakdown Structure (WBS).

Kerzner, H. 2009. *Project Management: A Systems Approach to Planning, Scheduling, and Controlling* – Tenth Edition. New York: John Wiley & Sons.

Larman, C. 2007. *Agile and Iterative Development: A Manager's Guide.* Boston, MA: Adison Wesley.

Maxwell, J. 2007. *Talent is never enough.* Nashville, TN: Thomas Nelson, Inc. (Spanish version).

Project Management Institute. 1987. *The Project Management Body of Knowledge (PMBOK®)*. Newtown Square, PA: Project Management Institute.

Project Management Institute. 1996. *A Guide to the Project Management Body of Knowledge (PMBOK® Guide)*. Newtown Square, PA: Project Management Institute.

Project Management Institute. 2006. *Practice Standard for Work Breakdown Structures*—Second Edition. Newtown Square, PA: Project Management Institute.

Project Management Institute. 2007. *Practice Standard for Scheduling*—Second Edition. Newtown Square, PA: Project Management Institute.

Project Management Institute. 2013. *A Guide to the Project Management Body of Knowledge (PMBOK® Guide)*—Fifth Edition. Newtown Square, PA: Project Management Institute.

Web References:

www.quotationspage.com
www.wikipedia.com

Web Resources:

www.buchtik.com	Contact the author
www.criticaltools.com	WBS Chart Pro™ software
www.freemind.sourceforge.net	Free Mind software
www.ibm.com	IBM Rational Portfolio Manager
www.matchware.com	MindView® software
www.microsoft.com	Microsoft® Office software products and WBS Modeler
www.mindject.com	MindManager®
www.oracle.com	Primavera® P6™
www.qpmusa.com/WBS-Director.html	WBS Director add-in
www.pmi.org	PMI's Agile Community of Practice
http://www.scrumalliance.org/	

About the Author

Liliana Buchtik, PMP, PMI-RMP, is a recognized project management author, speaker, and specialist. She is the author of the PMI-published *Secrets to Mastering the WBS in Real-World Projects,* and of *Secrets to Mastering Risk Management in Real-World Projects.* She is president of buchtik global®, a firm that provides project management training and consulting services globally, remotely or on-site.

She works with leading organizations like the *Project Management Institute* (PMI), based in the United States, where she worked for five years as an Information Technology (IT) project manager, facilitator at PMI Mega Certification Events where PMP exam questions are created, and as PMI's Latin American Representative. She is also an advisor for the Inter-American Development Bank (IDB) from Washington DC, USA, on program risk management for a 200 million-dollar five-year program - *Health Mesoamerica 2015* - funded by Bill & Melinda Gates Foundation, Carlos Slim Health Institute, and eight Latin American governments. She also teaches at international universities and business schools in Europe and Latin America. Liliana brings more than 15 years of experience from diverse management and project management positions in the IT and business fields, either in private or not-for-profit sectors, as well as in the government. She has also trained in the mining, construction and many other industries, including the risk management team of the biggest Latin American civil engineering Latin American program, the Panama Canal Expansion Program. She provides services in English and Spanish.

She is a specialist in PMI standards and has participated in the translations for *A Guide to the Project Management Body of Knowledge (PMBOK® Guide),* which is recognized as the global standard for the profession. She is a speaker at the largest project management events. Her articles have been featured in the most important magazines in the profession, like *PM Network®* and *MundoPM.* She served as an international correspondent for *PMForum* and *PM World Today* and has been recognized her for her outstanding support of the profession.

Liliana held key volunteer positions with PMI at international, regional, and national levels including being a member of the *PMI Ethics Appeal Committee.* She was the first PMI community mentor for Southern Latin America, integrated the first PMI Component Mentor Program Advisory Group, and was the president of the PMI Montevideo, Uruguay Chapter. She graduated from the PMI Leadership Institute Master Class in the United States. Liliana holds a bachelor's degree in Information Systems Analysis from ORT University, and has a diploma in managing people from ISEDE School of Business. Liliana is a native of Uruguay.

Reach her at liliana@buchtik.com or at www.Buchtik.com

Join the WORK BREAKDOWN STRUCTURE LinkedIn Group to discuss WBS related topics with peers and share questions and insights with readers about this book.